JourneyThrough®

Proverbs

50 Daily Insights from God's Word by **David Cook**

Foreword

The late Billy Graham, one of the greatest evangelists of the 20th century, used to read five Psalms each day, finishing the book in a month. He said the book of Psalms taught him about how to get along with God. Along with the Psalms, Graham also read one chapter of Proverbs each day. The book of Proverbs, he said, taught him about how to get along with his neighbours.

The book of Proverbs is a guidebook to the people of God on how they should live wisely and avoid making fools of themselves in life. Over the next 50 days, as you explore this almost 3,000-year-old book of ancient wisdom, you will no doubt be surprised by its contemporary relevance. God's instruction for life does not date: it neither depreciates nor improves with age; it is perfect forever.

I trust this title in the *Journey Through Series* will be a step on the path of your becoming a regular, careful, prayerful reader—and doer—of God's Word.

David Cook

We're glad you've decided to join us on a journey into a deeper relationship with Jesus Christ!

For over 50 years, we have been known for our daily Bible reading notes, *Our Daily Bread*. Many readers enjoy the pithy, inspiring, and relevant articles that point them to God and the wisdom and promises of His unchanging Word.

Building on the foundation of *Our Daily Bread*, we have developed this devotional series to help believers spend time with God in His Word, book by book. We trust this daily meditation on God's Word will draw you into a closer relationship with Him through our Lord and Saviour, Jesus Christ.

How to use this resource

READ: This book is designed to be read alongside God's Word as you journey with Him. It offers explanatory notes to help you understand the Scriptures in fresh ways.

REFLECT: The questions are designed to help you respond to God and His Word, letting Him change you from the inside out.

RECORD: The space provided allows you to keep a diary of your journey as you record your thoughts and jot down your responses.

An Overview

King Solomon, who reigned over Israel between 970 and 931 BC, was the main contributor to the book of Proverbs. He was responsible for the long section on wisdom (chapters 1–9) and the pithy proverbs in 10:1–22:16. The proverbs in 22:17–24:34 were adapted from wise men outside Israel. This section is followed by more of Solomon's proverbs (25:1–29:27).

We know nothing about Agur, whose fascinating proverbs follow in chapter 30, and little of King Lemuel, who was neither a king of Israel nor of Judah but who had a wise mother whose oracle he passes on in 31:1–8. The epilogue, 31:9–31, commends the woman of wisdom. This accolade has been given to Ruth (Ruth 3:11), linking it with the book of Ruth, which follows Proverbs in the Hebrew canon.

Proverbs' key theme, that "the fear of the LORD is the beginning of knowledge" (1:7, 9:10), reminds us that true knowledge and wisdom can be found only in a relationship of reverence and respect for God. To be truly wise is to revere God and to live according to His Word.

The Structure of Proverbs

1:1–7	Trials, blessings, temptation, religion, and wisdom
1:8–9:18	How faith integrates with action
10:1–22:16	How speech and wise living determine the course of our lives
22:17–24:34	A call to be obedient to God, and to turn away from the world
25:1–29:27	Dangers of greed and importance of patience and prayer
30:1–33	Sayings of Agur
31:1–9	Sayings of King Lemuel
31:10–31	Conclusion: The woman of wisdom

Key Verse

"The fear of the LORD is the beginning of knowledge, but fools despise wisdom and instruction." —Proverbs 1:7

Day 1

Read Proverbs 1:1–7

Solomon, introduced as the major author of the book of Proverbs (1:1), is the son of David. He was the king of Israel who asked God for wisdom—and was given it to such a degree that other kings sent envoys to hear it and the Queen of Sheba was overwhelmed by it (1 Kings 3:6–9, 4:29–34, 10:6–9).

Unfortunately, Solomon was eventually led astray by his many foreign wives (1 Kings 11:1–13). Clearly, merely knowing what is right is no substitute for doing it!

Solomon wrote 3,000 proverbs and 1,005 songs (1 Kings 4:32). In the book of Proverbs, we have his moral lessons and wisdom. This book will give insight and understanding (Proverbs 1:2), and wisdom to do what is right, just, and fair (v. 3). To the simple, it will give prudence (v. 4); to the young, it will give knowledge and discretion (v. 4); to the wise, it will give learning (v. 5); and to the discerning, it will give guidance (v. 5–6). Whichever category you fit into, this book is for you; it will inform your mind and mould your life.

But Proverbs is not just a book about gaining wisdom. The key to the book is verse 7, which notes that "the fear of the LORD is the beginning of knowledge". **This means revering God and remembering that it is He who created and redeemed us, recognising His complete power and authority over everything, and acknowledging our total dependence on Him.**

All knowledge come from either observation of creation or revelation by the Creator. But observation will not answer questions about what the Creator is like, why He made creation, how He is known, who we are, and what our purpose is; these questions can be answered only by revelation, which gives us God's big picture. We are thus called to listen to what He says, for that will give us the key to true knowledge.

On the other hand, fools—not necessarily the unintelligent—are those who reject God's authority, despise His revelation, and refuse the discipline of His knowledge (v. 7).

ThinkThrough

We are told Proverbs will benefit four types of people: the simple, the young, the wise, and the discerning (1:4–5). Which type might you be, and what can you gain from the book of Proverbs?

Proverbs 1 suggests that there are two ways to live: like the wise who fear the Lord, listen to His revelation, and live by His Word; or the fool who rejects God's wisdom and instruction, and depends on his own observation. How would you respond?

Day 2

Read Proverbs 1:8–33

Since the very beginning in the garden of Eden, two voices have been heard in Scripture: the voice of the Creator, and the contrary voice of the devil. In this section of Proverbs, we hear the two voices again. Both are speaking to "my son" (Proverbs 1:10), the young man.

One is the voice of sinful men (v. 10), the simple (v. 22), and the mockers (v. 22). This voice is enticing: it appeals to the young man to disregard consequences and pursue ill-gotten gains (vv. 11–13), and to throw in his lot with the wrong company (v. 14).

But the other voice—that of the wise parent (vv. 8–9) and also of Lady Wisdom (v. 20)—exposes the scheme and reveals it for what it really is: a trap (vv. 17–18) that will eventually cost people their own lives (v. 19).

Wisdom always shows the true reality: it cuts through lies and warns against submitting to temptation. It urges the young and simple to listen to and obey the right instruction (v. 8), and not to give in to the voice of sinful men (v. 10). Wisdom says: Consider the consequences! If we listen to this voice, we will enter its haven of safety (v. 33) but if we resist, we will suffer the consequence of our actions (v. 31). Wisdom calls us to fear the Lord (v. 29), but stubborn resistance will only lead to destruction (v. 32).

Wisdom's voice reminds us of the voice of Jesus Christ, God's wisdom in the flesh. Jesus reveals the truth of what God is like and how He intends humanity to live. He calls us to leave our naiveté and mockery (v. 22), and to repent.

This is a stark warning. Jesus Christ shows us the way to know God and to live in friendship with Him. To live any other way—no matter how enticing it may seem—is ultimately destructive. The fool hates knowledge and does not fear the Lord (v. 29), but the wise listens and fears the Lord—it is he who will find a secure and untroubled haven (v. 33).

ThinkThrough

Two voices speak
in Proverbs 1:8–33,
but only one is to be
obeyed. How can
you identify them
and obey the
right one?

What does Proverbs
1:8–33 say about the
fool's future? Is it his
fault or his fate? Pray
for wisdom not only
to know the right
path, but also to
walk on it.

Day 3

Read Proverbs 2

In Proverbs 2, we read words of encouragement from a father to a son, urging him to reflect on his commands and why he should obey them (vv. 1–2).

In verses 1–8, there are three "ifs": "if you accept my words" (v. 1); "if you call out for insight" (v. 3); and "if you look for [understanding] as for silver" (v. 4). If these things are done, the result is gaining an understanding of the fear of the Lord and knowledge of God (v. 5).

Wisdom is a gift of God (v. 6) as well as a result of searching, listening, and applying. **Human effort is involved but ultimately, wisdom is God's to give.** In the same way, God also gives success and protection (vv. 7–8). To see things the way God sees them, and to live wisely acknowledging that all we have is from God, is a very great blessing.

Wisdom will help us in three main ways:

• First, it gives us the discernment to distinguish between the right path to walk, and the dark one to avoid (vv. 12–15).

• Second, it reveals reality and brings the true consequences of actions to light, so that we can see a seemingly attractive offer for what it really is (vv. 16–19). Wisdom enables us to see through the seductive words of the adulterous woman, and to recognise that behind the veneer of attractiveness lies a path that leads to death (vv.18–19). It shows us that God's way is the foundation of life.

• Third, it leads to the blessing of living in God's land forever (vv. 20–21). The unfaithful and the wicked, on the other hand, have a very bleak future (v. 22). Notice that there are only two options! The son who listens to his wise father and comes to fear the Lord will escape the dark path and house (v. 18) which lead to death, and enjoy life in the land which God promises His people forever.

Wisdom is to be passionately sought and yet, it is also God's gift (James 1:5). What would this mean for your pursuit of wisdom?

God's wisdom gives discernment as well as knowledge of the consequences of our actions. How can these benefits of wisdom be helpful to you?

Day 4

Read Proverbs 3:1–12

Whenever God gives a command, He accompanies the command with a reason to obey. He never says "what" without saying "why".

In today's passage, there are six commands. Six times the wise father directs his son, each time giving a reason to obey and showing God's response to obedience. The commands—to continue embracing wisdom—tell us much about what the wise life involves:

- Remembering God's authoritative commands (Proverbs 3:1).

- Practising the covenant characteristics of love and faithfulness (v. 3).

- Trusting in the Lord's revelation and not in our own powers of understanding (v. 5), thus acknowledging His authority (v. 6).

- Revering Him and shunning the dark path (v. 7).

- Trusting the Lord and honouring Him in the giving of our wealth (v. 9).

- Recognising our need for correction and discipline, which God graciously gives in love (vv. 11–12).

The "whys" accompanying these commands include the promise of a long life (v. 2), a good reputation (v. 4), guidance from God (v. 6), physical nourishment (v. 8), reward for labour (v. 10), and spiritual maturity (v. 12; see also Hebrews 12:10).

Typical of wisdom literature in the Bible, these outcomes are generalisations rather than ironclad promises. Yet they are generally true—a life lived consistently by God's Word and marked by love, faithfulness, and openness to correction is most conducive to healthy productivity.

At the same time, the presence or absence of these results cannot be taken as an absolute indicator of a person's spiritual state or health. As Psalm 73 and the story of Job show, many will grapple with exceptions to these generalisations, raising questions like: Why do the wicked (or the fools, as Proverbs describes them) seem to do so well in life (see Psalm 73)? Why do the righteous (or the wise, according to Proverbs) suffer so appallingly (see Job)?

One answer is that the wise life pays dividends that may not always be physical or tangible; rather, the prosperity it gives is of eternal value. **Wisdom results in a contentment and maturity that none can take away.** Jesus Christ, the wisdom of God, is proof of that.

Proverbs 3:5–6
says we are to trust
wholeheartedly
in the Lord. What
do you think this
involves?

Reflect on what
Proverbs 3:11–12
and Hebrews 12:5–6
say about God's
discipline. How
can you treasure
godly rebuke and
correction?

Day 5

Read Proverbs 3:13–20

In this passage, the first of many beatitudes in Proverbs, we hear echoes of Psalm 1, Psalm 119, and Matthew 5. The one who finds wisdom finds true happiness!

Wisdom's inestimable value is described in Proverbs 3:14–15: "more profitable than silver" (v. 14), "yields better returns than gold" (v. 14), and "more precious than rubies" (v. 15). Wisdom offers both quantity and quality of life: she distributes gifts of long life—a sign of God's blessing—honour, and wealth (v. 16), and her paths are pleasant and peaceful (v. 17).

The reference to wisdom being a "tree of life" (v. 18) takes us back to the garden of Eden (Genesis 2:9). Access to this tree of life was lost when Adam and Eve listened to the serpent's voice. In the Bible, the "tree of life" often represents a fruitful, blessed life (see Proverbs 11:28–30, 13:12).

Wisdom's part in creation is described in 3:19–20: the wisdom of God is the source of a well-ordered creation. If God had created the order and rhythms of life through wisdom, then the best orientation we can have for living in God's world is to know this wisdom by which He created the world.

For Old Testament believers, this wisdom was to be found in the fear of the Lord (1:7). For us today, it means following Jesus Christ, the wisdom of God (1 Corinthians 1:24, 30). For "through him all things were made" (John 1:3) and "all things have been created through him and for him" (Colossians 1:16).

To try to live happily in God's world without reference to Jesus Christ—through whom and by whom the world was made—is a hopeless quest. Jesus is the wisdom who promises us abundant life (John 10:10).

Proverbs 3 reflects a father's loving and passionate concern that his son recognises the value of wisdom and sets out on its path. Knowing wisdom is both a gift and a task. In the same way, Jesus is God's greatest gift to us; however, growing in Christ also involves prayerful discipline, listening to the Word of God, rejecting the serpent's voice, and walking the narrow path.

What does wisdom offer us in terms of the quantity and quality of life? What do you think is the key to living a life of wisdom?

How would you respond to the fact that growing in wisdom is both a gift and a task?

Day 6

Read Proverbs 3:21–35

The father continues urging his son to keep pursuing wisdom by showing why God desires it and what it produces. In Proverbs 3:21, he adds to the emphasis by pleading with his son not to let these twin aspects of wisdom out of his sight: sound judgment or common sense, and discretion or discernment.

These are the fruits of wisdom—the ability to act shrewdly in response to a problem, and the ability to discern and think through the possible consequences before carrying out an action. In other words, wisdom causes us to stop and think things through. The benefits of doing this are outlined in verses 22–25: when we live by God's ways, He will watch over us (v. 26).

Such sound judgment and discernment will always show themselves in the integrity of relationships: the wise will neither withhold nor defer doing good to others, will do no harm, will make no baseless accusations, and will not envy the violent (vv. 27–31). In other words, the wise will be diligent members of the community, contributing to its peace and harmony.

The Lord himself stands behind these exhortations: He detests the perverse (v. 32), curses the wicked (v. 33), and mocks the mocker (v. 34), as these are contrary to His character and will. At the same time, He shares with the upright (v. 32), blesses the righteous (v. 33), and gives grace to the humble (v. 34; see James 4:6). The son is urged to choose the right path.

The father concludes with one last warning in verse 35: the wise will inherit an honourable reputation, while the fool will ultimately be shamed.

Prayerful, considered living; addressing issues with a commitment to the integrity and priority of God's Word; thinking clearly through the consequences of a proposal—all these are aspects of the wise life. Do not let them out of your sight (v. 21)!

ThinkThrough

How can you apply sound judgment and discernment to the issues you face today?

Pray through Proverbs 3:21–22. How can you make more effort to keep to this pattern of living? Ask God to help you preserve these elements of wisdom, and to not lose sight of them.

Day 7

Read Proverbs 4

Proverbs 4 is divided into three sections, each continuing the pattern of addressing "my son" (vv. 1, 10, 20).

The first section (vv. 1–9) stresses the supremacy of wisdom: she is to be embraced at all costs (v. 7), and cherishing her will pay a rich dividend (vv. 8–9). The appeal is made across generations: the father was taught by his own father (vv. 3–4), and he now passes the exhortation on to the third generation, saying: "do not forget my words or turn away from them" (v. 5). These words have stood the test of time.

The second section (vv. 10–19) repeats the picture of the two paths. The son is to stay on the path of wisdom (v. 11) and avoid the path of the wicked (vv. 14–15); the father is setting the son on the straight path (v. 11).

The lifestyle of the wicked is wholeheartedly evil; they are so addicted to doing evil that they cannot sleep without it (v. 16). Their staple diet is wickedness and violence (v. 17). One path is gloriously bright, and the other, ever-deepening darkness (vv. 18–19).

Note the commands to "listen" (v. 10), "hold on" (v. 13), "do not set foot" (v. 14), and "avoid" (v. 15). The wise life means always being on the alert and making disciplined, conscious decisions to pursue wisdom.

The third section (vv. 20–27) encourages the young man to check his spiritual health, attitude, and behaviour. He is to guard his heart and his whole inner life, especially his thoughts (v. 23). He is to rid his mouth of perversity (v. 24), for "the mouth speaks what the heart is full of" (Matthew 12:34). He is to keep his eyes focused on the straight path (Proverbs 4:25)—the way of wisdom, the way of the Lord. This will keep his feet on firm ground and from drifting into evil (vv. 26–27).

Proverbs 4 reminds us that being on the path of wisdom is not a one-off choice, but a lifetime of saying "yes" to wisdom and "no" to the way of the wicked. As Paul reminds Titus, the grace of God "teaches us to say 'No' to ungodliness and worldly passions, and to live self-controlled, upright and godly lives in this present age" (Titus 2:12).

What are the benefits that the wise will enjoy?

Check your own thoughts, words, and actions. What do you find about your heart, mouth, eyes, and feet in the light of Proverbs 4:23–27?

Day 8

Read Proverbs 5

As I write this devotion, there are numerous reports of adultery circulating in the Australian media. One is about a senior political leader who has been sexually involved with a woman to whom he is not married. Interestingly, the reports refer to this as an "affair" and "sexual relations", but none have called it for what it is—adultery. Adultery represents the breaking of a vow between a husband and wife to commit themselves to each other unconditionally and exclusively.

The other thing I have noticed is that everyone affected by adultery is hurt by it. When there is adultery, no one wins. Also, adultery always promises happiness, but always fails to deliver. No one is better off, for there is no more consistent liar than adultery: it breaks every promise.

Proverbs 5 contains a warning against sexual immorality, using adultery as an example. The father tells the son to be on the alert for the seductress and her temptations. The adulteress is appealing (v. 3), but following her will end in bitterness and injury (v. 4). Her bed, for all its attractiveness, is a grave (v. 5). To go to her will bring about great waste (vv. 9–10) and regret (vv. 11–14).

Adultery, and all forms of sexual immorality, comes with a dreadful price tag. God knows it, and that is why He says: Don't do it! (Exodus 20:14; 1 Corinthians 6:18–20).

In Proverbs 5:15–19, the language becomes very beautiful, even erotic, rather like the Song of Songs. There is satisfaction and joy in being captivated by the wife of one's youth. She is one's own cistern, a fountain, a loving doe, a graceful deer. Here is the passionate, fulfilling, sexual morality of the wise, all based on marital faithfulness.

Sexual foolishness cannot be hidden from God and will be judged by Him (v. 21). Immorality will trap and enslave those who do evil (v. 22), lead them astray, and ultimately destroy them (v. 23).

Perhaps Proverbs 5 has been included because foolishness is never more clearly on display than in sexual immorality. The father uses these warnings to snap his son out of complacency and remind him of the dangers of giving in to temptation.

The fruit of wisdom—as seen in faithful, loyal love and commitment in marriage—is universally recognised as the right path. Again, we see that when God's Word is listened to and obeyed, society, the home, and the individual will all thrive.

ThinkThrough

We've seen how
God never tells
us "what" to do
without telling us
"why". What reasons
does Proverbs 5
give to explain His
command to walk in
sexual purity?

Pray for God's help
in living a life of
sexual purity.

Day 9

Read Proverbs 6

Proverbs 6 has four distinct sections, on financial prudence (vv. 1–3), diligence (vv. 6–11), troublemakers (vv. 12–19), and adultery (vv. 20–35).

Verses 1–3 urge the son to be prudent in financial affairs. Entering an agreement to be a guarantor for a neighbour's debt (v. 1) means becoming responsible for another person's foolish choices; such an agreement is a trap (v. 2; see Proverbs 17:18). The father urges the son to lose no time and spare no effort in liberating himself from this snare (vv. 3–5).

Verses 6–11 urge the son to observe the ant and learn diligence from it. The industrious ant is a model of wise activity (vv. 6–8; see Proverbs 30:25); its hard work (vv. 6–7) is contrasted with the sluggard who finds every excuse to rest (v. 10; see also Proverbs 24:30–34). One results in ample provision (v. 8) while the other results in scarcity (v. 11).

Verses 12–19 warn against the wicked and the troublemaker, who has a perverse mouth (v. 12) and devious behaviour that come from evil intentions (vv. 13–14)—such a person will ultimately be destroyed (v. 15). In this context, the writer introduces seven things which God hates (vv. 16–19). Heading the list is pride. **Note that wickedness includes works of the hands, feet, tongue, and heart.** Finally, we are told that God detests the one who "stirs up conflict in the community" (v. 19).

The final section, verses 20–35, stresses the vital importance of resisting adultery; a repetition of the warnings given in Proverbs 5 to 7. The writer makes it clear that adultery is a process that begins with lustful eyes (v. 25), and also notes that while relations with a prostitute (v. 26) are bad enough, taking another man's wife—even if it's at her initiative (v. 26)—is even worse.

This chapter's warning against adultery stresses the consequences of adultery (vv. 27–29) more than in previous chapters. While theft may be understood when there are desperate circumstances (vv. 30–31), adultery will earn nothing but destruction (v. 32), shame, and disgrace (v. 33), as well as a husband's fury (v. 34).

Note that in a civil society, an adulterer is to be named and shamed (v. 33). Any other response is indicative of a society's decadent attitude of compromise and tolerance.

Do you tolerate any of the things God loathes (Proverbs 6:16–19)? Pray that God will help you clothe yourself in His qualities.

Why do you think the writer returns to the issue of adultery? What does this section say which hasn't been said before?

Day 10

Read Proverbs 7

When it comes to the moment of enticement, when reason and passion compete, it is tragic that passion is often the victor. The author—Solomon—himself is a sobering example: even though he wrote all these proverbs on wisdom and sexual purity, "King Solomon . . . loved many foreign women" (1 Kings 11:1).

In today's passage, the father urges his son to hold on tightly to the wise words that will keep him from the words of the seductress (Proverbs 7:1–5). This chapter then takes the form of a narrative featuring a youth (v. 7), a seductress (v. 10), and a list of victims (v. 26).

The young man is described as naive (v. 7)—exactly the type of person for whom the book of Proverbs is written (1:4). He is found in the company of other young and simple men, walking near the woman's corner at dusk (7:7–9)—perhaps not the wisest place nor time to be, where temptation lurks.

Verses 10–21 tell us what happens next. The brazen woman, who has crafty intent, comes out to offer the youth food, a perfume-covered bed, and a place where they can "drink deeply of love till morning" (v. 18). She tells him that he is the special one she has been looking for (v. 15),

and succeeds in leading him astray (v. 21) into a one-night stand with no strings attached. Why not, when it seems so good!

Verses 22–23 are filled with pathos. The ox is led to the slaughter, the deer to the noose, the bird to the snare. **That which seemed so good and inviting is a tragic entrapment.** A young man, a crafty woman, and now, another victim added to the list!

And so the father warns his son to beware the consequences of his actions (v. 24). There are always strings attached, he says. Look more carefully, scratch the silky surface, peel back the smooth talk, and smell beyond the perfumed bedroom—the pungent odour of death is there. Can't you smell it, my son?

Don't let your heart or body go to the woman's house (v. 25), the wise teacher warns, because you don't want your name to appear on her long list of victims: "Many are the victims she has brought down; her slain are a mighty throng" (v. 26).

Verse 27 summarises the warning. The woman's house, as popular and attractive as it may seem, is an expressway to the place of the dead. Using a variety of metaphors, the wise teacher and father urges the young man to look beyond her seductive appeal and to consider the consequences, so that when reason and passion compete, wisdom will be his sister and understanding his relative (v. 4).

How can we apply the lessons of Proverbs 7 in our lives today, particularly in recognising and avoiding tempting situations?

What would the dangers and consequences of giving in to a seductress— as outlined in Proverbs 7—look like in today's world?

Day 11

Read Proverbs 8:1–21

We first met Lady Wisdom on Day 2 (Proverbs 1:20), when she spoke briefly (vv. 22–33). Now, having heard about the lure of the seductress in Proverbs 5, 6:20–35, and 7:6–27, we hear from Lady Wisdom again.

Proverbs 8 stresses Lady Wisdom's accessibility. She is not hidden, but stands on the heights, at intersections, and at major entry points (vv. 2–3). **A stark contrast to the seductress' secretive and deceptive ways, Lady Wisdom is open and honest.** She is also available to everyone (v. 4), and the simple, the naive, and the foolish— who are gullible and easily misled— would do well to listen to her (v. 5).

Verses 6–9 show the ethical value of Lady Wisdom's speech, while verses 10–11 extol their preciousness. We are thus to "listen" (v. 6) and to "choose" her instructions (v. 10).

In a world of much talk and twitter, how refreshing it is to be exhorted to simply listen! In a world in which material possessions are deemed all-important, how surprising it is to be urged to pursue that which is non-material—wisdom!

These are the qualities with which Lady Wisdom is much at home: prudence, knowledge, and discretion (v. 12). She distances herself from pride, arrogance, evil, and perversity (v. 13)—all traits of the foolish life. The qualities of wisdom make for successful leadership (vv. 14–16). Wisdom will sometimes also lead to wealth (vv. 18–21), as in the case of Solomon. Remember, however, that he sought wisdom first, and wealth came only as its companion (1 Kings 3:13).

We saw in Proverbs 2:6 (Day 3) that wisdom is a gift of God. Here, we also see Lady Wisdom giving gifts— she rewards those who love and seek her (8:17), and she provides precious fruit to passionate, single-minded suitors (v. 19).

Wisdom's appeal is a familiar one: "Everyone who asks receives; the one who seeks finds; and to the one who knocks, the door will be opened" (Matthew 7:8).

God's wisdom is freely available to you. How would you apply it in your life?

How much do prudence (shrewd thinking), knowledge (understanding reality through the lens of God's revelation), and discretion (making the right choices) mark your life?

Day 12

Read Proverbs 8:22–36

Wisdom sets out clearly her supreme credentials in her autobiography: she is born or generated of the Lord himself, and she is around before the creation of the world, before the oceans, land, and the heavens were created (Proverbs 8:22–27). She is constantly at God's side, delights in His presence, and rejoices in creation and humankind (vv. 30–31). Who is Wisdom? She is an attribute of God, who is all-wise.

Many believe Proverbs 8:22–36 describes the pre-incarnate Lord Jesus, who never acted apart from wisdom as His constant companion. However, more can be said of Jesus than is said here of Wisdom.

John 1:3 describes Jesus this way: "Through him all things were made", and in Colossians 1:15-17, we read that Jesus is the agent of creation and the reason for its being. Though Wisdom was with God at creation, nowhere in Proverbs 8 does she claim to be the Creator.

Throughout my ministry I have been involved in many building projects, I have seen buildings being constructed from plan to completion, and I rejoiced in the progress, but I was not the builder. Creation is a divine accomplishment. God acts with wisdom, and He is the Creator who creates through and for His Son (Colossians 1:16).

God the Father is guided by wisdom. God the Son embodies wisdom; all He does, especially at the cross, is truly wise. God the Spirit makes that same wisdom available to us.

God does all things with wisdom, and so should we! **Amazingly, those who seek Wisdom will find her and be blessed (Proverbs 8: 32–36).** She is available to all, not just for the elites. However, to qualify for such an exalted companion, we must listen to her and her instruction (vv. 32–34). As church reformer Martin Luther once put it: "Ears are the only organs of the Christian."[1] Romans 10:17 also reminds us that "faith comes from hearing the message".

Will you seek Wisdom, "watching daily at my doors, waiting at my doorway" (Proverbs 8:34)? The best way to begin the day is to prayerfully read God's Word, hear from Him, and then join the kings, rulers, princes and nobles (vv. 15–16) who are guided by Wisdom, and blessed by her.

[1] Timothy George, *Theology of the Reformers* (Nashville, TN: Broadman Press, 1988).

ThinkThrough

The key to blessing is to listen to Lady Wisdom's voice—that is, God's wisdom. Where do you think this wisdom can be found? How can we take Wisdom's invitation seriously?

How can we apply God's wisdom to our daily life and routine?

Day 13

Read Proverbs 9:1–6

A chiasm is a literary technique that inverts a phrase with a following phrase, often using repeated words or ideas. For example: "When the going gets tough, the tough get going." Through symmetry, chiasms help to emphasise contrast or a central point that may be inserted between the two phrases. The Bible has a number of such chiasms, and Proverbs 9 is one of them.

In this final chapter urging the reader to choose between two women, Lady Wisdom (vv. 1–6) and Madame Folly (vv. 13–18), the chiasm focuses attention on the verses in the middle—verses 7–12, which contrast the mocker (vv. 7–8) and the wise (vv. 9–10). This puts the central focus of the chapter on verse 10: the fear of the Lord.

In verses 1–6, we see the characteristics of Lady Wisdom's invitation to her substantial, perfect house (v. 1): there is a sumptuous meal of meat and wine on offer (v. 2), and maids broadcasting an invitation to the naive and simple (vv. 3–4). It is an invitation to leave naivety and to walk in the way of the righteous—a meal that will lead to life (v. 6).

Consider the contrast between Lady Wisdom's offering and Madame Folly's invitation (vv. 13–18), which is also directed at the simple and naive (v. 16) but involves enjoying the sweet pleasures of a stolen meal that will lead to death (vv. 17–18). We will look at it in greater detail later, on Day 15. Lady Wisdom's words remind us of another who invites His hearers, not to a meal but to himself: "Come to me, all you who are weary and burdened, and I will give you rest" (Matthew 11:28).

Here is Lady's Wisdom's generous invitation to all who are willing to listen, even if they are simple and naive: **come and partake of a sumptuous meal; repent, leave your simple ways, and you will live.**

ThinkThrough

Why don't more people accept Lady Wisdom's generous invitation to pursue wisdom and live?

What does it mean to "leave your simple ways" and "walk in the way of insight" (Proverbs 9:6)?

Day 14

Read Proverbs 9:7–12

Having briefly looked at the contrast between the two invitations by Lady Wisdom and Madame Folly, we now shift the focus of our attention to the verses in the centre of the chiasm. Today's passage contrasts the diners at each table.

Those who dine at Madame Folly's table (Proverbs 9:7–8) are characterised by an arrogance that does not appreciate correction or rebuke. They are so out of touch with the reality of their own state, thinking they have it all together, that they are offended at the very suggestion of the need for repentance. The corrective word invites abuse and hatred. Those who dine at Lady Wisdom's (vv. 8–9), on the other hand, are wise and know their need for correction. They welcome the rebuke and will learn from it.

The introduction to Proverbs promises that this book will bring addition to the wise (1:5–6). This is because the wise know how little they know and how deceptive their hearts can be (Jeremiah 17:9). They thus appreciate instruction and teaching, even rebuke and correction, as an act of love. Such people have this attitude because of their "fear of the LORD" (Proverbs 9:10)—a reverence for God that comes with acknowledging His sovereignty and holiness, being grateful for the privilege of being in a loving relationship with Him, and recognising that He is the true source of wisdom and knowledge.

Fear of the Lord leads to wisdom, which in turn gives the blessing of a long life (v. 11). This is a generalisation: while verse 11 is not promising literal longevity, a wise life that is lived in accordance with God's will, purpose, and creation order is conducive to a long one. The wise person who dines at the table of Lady Wisdom will be rewarded just as the fool will lose (v. 12); this is something that we take responsibility for as an individual. Our decision to pursue wisdom or folly builds our character—which, as Bible commentator Derek Kidner puts it, is something you "cannot borrow, lend or escape, for it is you".[2]

True wisdom is both a gift of God as well as the result of seeking and searching.

Keeping a level head through prayerfulness; recognising the voice of Lady Wisdom and avoiding that of Madame Folly; considering the consequences of our actions; revering God's words and seeing things through His lens; repenting of our sins; and living according to God's will and purposes in creation—this is the truly wise life!

[2] Derek Kidner, *Proverbs*, Tyndale Old Testament Commentaries (Downers Grove, IL: IVP Academic, 2009), 83.

Reflecting on the lessons learned in Proverbs 1–9, what reasons would you give a young disciple for following the path of wisdom?

How should we respond to correction and rebuke?

Day 15

Read Proverbs 9:13–18

Like Lady Wisdom, Madame Folly has also prepared a banquet for her guests. Those whom she invites are the same as those to whom Lady Wisdom calls out. "Let all who are simple come to my house!" she says to those who lack judgment (Proverbs 9:16, see v. 4).

Her invitation and advice, however, are antithetical to those of Lady Wisdom. While Lady Wisdom offers life (v. 6), Madame Folly offers only temporary satisfaction (v. 17). What she offers is forbidden—stolen water and food that has to be eaten in secret. This could be a metaphor for the sexual pleasure of adultery, which the writer of Proverbs warned against earlier (2:17, 5:15, 6:30–35, 7:18–19). Such stolen drink and food is sweet and delicious, as long as you don't think of the consequences.

Once again, keeping an eye firmly on reality, the writer describes those who eat with Madame Folly as being "deep in the realm of the dead" (9:18)—their actions will lead to death. This is what Madame Folly is inviting her guests to do: live for the moment; enjoy (for that is the only goal); and dismiss consequence, prudence, and discernment.

This section of Proverbs 1–9 begins with the promise of easy wealth (1:11–14) and is sprinkled throughout with the promise of easy sex. There is no consideration of the consequences beyond the pleasure of the night (7:18–20).

The shipwrecks of lives around us are evidence that many people have been attracted to and accepted Madame Folly's invitation. Many will probably tell you that given a chance to start over again, they would never have joined her for that meal. On the other hand, none who eat with Lady Wisdom will ever regret eating her food.

Proverbs 9 concludes the section beginning at 1:8 (see Overview, page 5), and it explicitly commends wisdom. What a chapter this is! It puts in stark contrast the benefits of life and understanding versus death and the depths of the grave. All of us are hearing two invitations—one to partake of wisdom and the other of folly. What a privilege it is to eat Lady Wisdom's food. Pray that you will never be enticed by Madame Folly's poisoned banquet!

How might Madame
Folly's invitation
look like in today's
context?

Take another look at
Proverbs 1–9. How
often does the writer
speak of the two
voices, ways, and
paths?

Day 16

Read Proverbs 5:1–6, 6:25–29, 7:6–27

n the first section of Proverbs (chapters 1–9), the writer writes as a father urging his son to avoid sexual temptation and adultery, and to be faithful if he is married. This issue is highlighted in these three passages, 5:1–23, 6:20–35, 7:1–27.

Sexual temptation is an ever-present issue in the life of all, especially the young. Today, some might even see the single who abstains from sexual activity and the married couple who remain faithful within marriage as oddities, relics of the past. The Bible encourages active, pleasurable sexual activity within a marriage between man and woman, but warns against other kinds of sexual activity—such as that outside of marriage.

The two women whom the young man meets are "the wife of your youth" (5:18) and the prostitute (6:26), who is also described as the adulteress (5:3) and the immoral woman (6:24). These two types of women compete for the attention of the young man, and parallel the two women, Wisdom and Folly, who compete for his spiritual, intellectual, emotional, and volitional loyalty.

The father urges his son to be faithful to his wife just as he had urged his son to dine continually at Lady Wisdom's table. The prostitute and adulteress are to be avoided, as is Madame Folly.

Like the devil himself, Folly and the prostitute are masters of subtle suggestion. They are always prowling around looking for victims to devour (5:3–4; 6:25; 7:10–12; see also 1 Peter 5:8). They seek to lure people into their trap—a trap that leads to death (Proverbs 5:5; 6:27–28; 7:22–23, 26–27).

The Bible makes clear that the people of God are to resist Folly and the adulteress, and to follow Wisdom, who leads them in the way of God (see James 4:7).

How do we resist one and embrace the other? Proverbs makes it clear in 9:10: Fear the Lord! **Reverence for God and His Word is the essential sword which God has provided for this battle against sexual temptation.**

Church reformer John Calvin once wrote: "God's speaking is opposed to all the clamours of Satan . . . The only unfailing security for the faithful is to acquiesce in God's word."

ThinkThrough

In which part of your life might you be vulnerable to sexual temptation?

What strategies can you employ to resist the call of Folly and temptations of the adulteress?

Day 17

Read Proverbs 10:1–14

When I preach and apply the truth of a Bible passage for my listeners, I often point out the impossible opposite application of the passage. For example, the Bible says: "All have sinned" (Romans 3:23); the antithesis would be: "No one has sinned."

In Proverbs 10, there are 32 proverbs covering different subjects, but their form is the same. Each proverb has two lines—a couplet in which the second line re-states the first, but in the opposite direction. This is a common form of Hebrew poetry called antithetical parallelism. Verse 1 is a good example. Note the opposites: the wise son brings joy, but the foolish son brings grief. The second line heightens the impact of the first by describing its devastating opposite.

The wide variety of topics involving wisdom can be seen in the diverse themes of this chapter. They include:

- ill-gotten treasure (v. 2)
- hunger (v. 3)
- laziness (vv. 4–5, 26)
- righteousness (vv. 6–7, 16, 24–25, 28, 30)
- the fear or way of the Lord (vv. 8, 17, 23, 27, 29)
- integrity (v. 9)
- the tongue (vv. 11, 13–14, 18–21, 31–32)

While it would be futile to look for a common theme in this chapter, the tongue appears to receive special attention. Jesus described the tongue as an indicator of the whole state of a person's inner life, for "the mouth speaks what the heart is full of" (Matthew 12:34). Proverbs 10 contrasts the words of the wise and foolish and notes how their fruit distinguishes them:

- The words of the wise refresh, encourage, and bring life, but the words of the fool discourage and destroy (v. 11).

- The words of the wise show discernment, but those of the fool are misguided and invite trouble and punishment (v. 13).

- The wise speak only when needed, preferring to store up their knowledge, but the fool comes to ruin because of his careless, ignorant talk (v. 14).

Our words not only reflect the state of our hearts, but also affect others profoundly, for good or ill. Little wonder that

Proverbs 12:18 compares words to swords; in fact, while the latter affects the body only, the former can affect the spirit. Sticks and stones may break my bones, but words can do even more harm!

Listen to your own words. What do they tell you about your heart?

Reflect on Jesus' wise use of His words. Pray that God will help you speak wisely today.

Day 18

Read Proverbs 10:15–32

In today's passage, we continue to look at the contrast between the words of the wise and those of the fool. Solomon compares their tongues, noting how judiciously they are used and their impact on both the listener and the speaker:

- The wise holds his tongue with discipline, but the fool's many words lead to sin (Proverbs 10:19).

- The words of the wise are valuable because they encourage and refresh, but those of the fool are useless because he is only interested in lies and slander, and has a wicked heart (vv. 18, 20).

- The words of the wise nourish their listeners, but the fool's words are empty, unable even to nourish himself (v. 21).

- The wise give good advice, but the fool's words are perverse and earn punishment (v. 31).

- The wise speak appropriately, but the fool says what is not acceptable (v. 32).

Verse 18: "Whoever conceals hatred with lying lips and spreads slander is a fool", stands out because it is not an antithetical parallelism like the other proverbs. Instead, it talks about how the fool not only conceals his hatred of someone by lying—perhaps by pretending to be a friend—but even slanders the person behind his back. The impact of a fool's words is a stark contrast to that of the words of the wise, which 10:11 refers to as a fountain of life. **When we speak to encourage, edify, or correct, we become a source of life and nourishment.** No wonder James described the tongue as a small but influential, potentially destructive member of our body (James 3:1–12).

Knowing when to speak and when to be silent is a key theme in Proverbs, especially in 10:15–32; the right use of the wise tongue is wonderfully enriching to all who hear its words.

Oh, be careful, little mouth,
what you say.
Oh, be careful, little mouth,
what you say.
For the Father up above is looking
down in love,
So be careful, little mouth,
what you say!

How can you speak more encouragingly today?

How can you ensure that your speech is inspired by the Holy Spirit?

Day 19

Read Proverbs 11

The book of Proverbs teaches us how to live wisely. And wise living starts with acknowledging that true knowledge begins with fearing the Lord (1:7).

Proverbs 11 begins with the observation that God is interested in the lives of His people, even in the way they conduct their business dealings (v. 1). There are no areas of our lives that are outside His interest or His rule! **The Lord delights in honesty in His people, for He is truth. He detests dishonesty, for there is no falsehood in Him.**

Honesty and using accurate weights (v. 1) reflect righteousness—a topic that dominates Proverbs 11. And righteousness comes when we are in the right with God; this shows itself in a new lifestyle that includes honesty (v. 1), humility (v. 2), integrity (v. 3), uprightness (v. 11), trustworthiness (v. 13), and blamelessness (v. 20). Such a lifestyle is a hallmark of God's grace and a life redeemed.

This chapter is full of contrasts, and verse 3 is a typical example. It compares the upright, who trust in the Lord and live by His ways, and the wicked, who are duplicitous. These two ways produce opposite results:

the first will receive the blessing of life, while the second will ultimately come to nothing (v. 19). All the wicked will find is death.

The righteous have hope of a future (vv. 4, 18, 19, 21, 23); this hope and sense of accountability drive their generosity (vv. 24–25) and give them a proper view of riches (v. 28). The people of God respond with kindness, not ruthlessness or cruelty (vv. 16–17), and do not hoard for themselves (v. 26). As preacher Charles Spurgeon once put it: "The smoke of the chimney is as solid as the comfort of riches."[3]

Proverbs 11 shows that all will be judged for their deeds (vv. 4, 6, 8, 19, 21, 23, 28, 31). The wise will be vindicated and delivered, while the wicked will be punished. Some of these consequences may be seen in their lifetimes (e.g. vv. 3, 5, 6, 17), while some will take place after (vv. 4, 7, 19, 21).

While Proverbs 11 does not say who is doing the judging, we know that God is the ultimate judge who will hold all to account (Genesis 18:25; Psalm 9:7–8). God, who is righteous, will bless the righteous and punish the wicked—if not in this life, then certainly after (Proverbs 11:21).

There is no area of our lives that are not under His Lordship. We cannot live one way in public and another in private; all parts of our lives are lived before Him.

[3] Charles Spurgeon, "A Drama in Five Acts", sermon no. 481, *Metropolitan Tabernacle Pulpit*, vol. 8 (1862), https://www.spurgeon.org/resource-library/sermons/a-drama-in-five-acts#flipbook/

ThinkThrough

List down what Proverbs 11 says about what God delights in and what He detests. How can this guide you in your attitude and in what you do?

Think about what this chapter says about wealth, kindness, the tongue, and hope. Which one is most relevant for you today?

Day 20

Read Proverbs 12

This chapter has many lessons and observations about wise and godly living. Let's take a closer look at a few of them:

One, the power of words to help or hurt—and the effect on the speaker himself—is a prominent theme (Proverbs 12:6, 13–14, 17–19, 22). Associated with this emphasis is the discretion to know when to speak and when to remain silent (v. 23). The wise seek to bless others and tell the truth (vv. 17–18), while the wicked seek to destroy and deceive (vv. 6, 17–18). The fool has an inflated view of his own knowledge (v. 15), while the wise know what they don't know and therefore listen to advice (v. 15).

Two, the importance of words is also seen in the observation that the Lord detests lies and deception; He delights in truth (v. 22). The apostle Paul describes Him as the God "who does not lie" (Titus 1:2).

Three, reality is more important than appearance (Proverbs 12:9). Better to appear to be a nobody but actually be a somebody, than have the appearance of being a somebody and yet have nothing. What a contrast this is to today's pressure to "put on an appearance"!

Four, the wise person recognises the need to be in right relationships, including with God's creation, and therefore cares for his animals (v. 10). Because a righteous person is concerned for those around him—including his pets and livestock—a person's attitude towards animals can reveal much about him. English social reformer Rowland Hill sums it up well: "I care not for a man's repentance if his dog and cat are not the better for it."

Five, self-control is another prominent theme (v. 16; see also 29:11). It is characterised by an insensitivity to insult and an ability to resist impulsive behaviour (see 13:3, 16). **Self-control—which comes from the Holy Spirit—is most evident when we are offended or find ourselves in a position where we want to ventilate our anger.**

Six, diligence and hard work is of great value (12:11, 14, 24, 27). Hard work brings reward; the lazy person will only end up trapped in forced labour (v. 24) and poverty (10:4). Proverbs 12:27 compares the efforts put in by the diligent and the lazy: one is too lazy even to cook what he has caught to feed himself, whereas the other does what is needed to fill himself. This could be a comparison between those who quit too soon, and those who persevere and see their projects to completion—and are rewarded for it.

What a privilege it is to receive such wisdom from the mind of God, revealed in these Scriptures! The righteous and wise learn from these observations and lessons. Will you apply them to your speech, attitude, and character today?

Proverbs 12:1 says that "whoever loves discipline loves knowledge", and "whoever hates correction is stupid". How does this apply to your own life?

How can you apply what Proverbs 12 teaches about the importance of words, putting on appearances, care for creation, self-control, and work attitude? Which is the most challenging for you?

Day 21

Read Proverbs 13:1–18

Proverbs 13:1–16 contains some of the most common themes of wisdom: righteous speech (vv. 2–3), diligence (v. 4), righteousness and integrity (vv. 5–6, 9), and attitude towards wealth (vv. 7–8, 11).

One prominent topic in this chapter, however, is about listening to and heeding wise advice and commands (vv. 1, 10, 13–14, 18). **Clearly, the first important action we need to take in our search for wisdom is to listen and obey.** The wise person's humility and willingness to listen (vv. 1, 10, 14) is thus contrasted with the mocker's stubbornness and deafness (vv. 1, 13). These two attitudes, with their associated deeds, will produce opposite outcomes—reward or punishment (v. 13). Those who listen to the words of the wise will find an abundant source of life, and avoid being trapped by the snares of evil (v. 14).

That's why verse 18 notes that those who heed correction will find the honour that comes from success, whereas those who ignore wisdom will not. Like the wise son, we need to heed the instructions (v. 1) in order to benefit from the book of Proverbs (1:4).

Like some young people, we may not recognise our need to listen, or we may listen to the wrong people— perhaps because our own peers are more influential or trendier than the wise. Listen to those who have your best interests at heart!

Let's take a quick look at the parts covering righteousness, pride, and wealth in Proverbs 13.

Verse 5: The righteous hate falsehood because they fear a God who detests lies (12:22), whereas the wicked indulge in lies and slander, which ultimately bring disgrace and shame upon themselves.

Verse 8: The rich may be disadvantaged by their wealth: they are more likely to be robbed, targeted, or held to ransom for their possessions. The poor, on the other hand, have a form of liberty because no one is interested in them. No wonder Ecclesiastes 5:10–12 notes that wealth will never bring ultimate satisfaction. The poor sleep well because they have no concern about thieves breaking in, but the rich are sleepless with worry.

Verse 10: Pride—or contempt for others' opinions—is an ever-present ingredient in every quarrel. A proud person listens to no-one, but a wise person is open to correction.

Verse 16: Wisdom and prudence— acting cautiously and circumspectly in all circumstances—are close friends. In contrast, the fool rejects advice and reacts impulsively, showing his folly through his actions.

[4] John Calvin, *Commentary on Harmony of the Evangelist, Matthew, Mark, and Luke,* trans. William Pringle (Edinburgh: Calvin Translation Society, 1845), 337–338.

Theologian John Calvin once said: "Where riches hold the dominion of heart, God has lost His authority . . . Covetousness makes us the slaves of the devil."[4] How would this apply to you?

How can you make sure you're listening to the right advice and commands?

Day 22

Read Proverbs 13:19–25

Spare the rod and spoil the child. Despite common belief, this familiar saying does not come from the Bible, but from 17th-century English poet Samuel Butler. It is likely, however, that the poet may have been thinking of Proverbs 13:24 when he coined the maxim: "Whoever spares the rod hates their children, but the one who loves their children is careful to discipline them."

Butler's saying seems to advocate corporal punishment, warning that not doing so will produce a badly-brought up child. But Proverbs gives a more complete picture of discipline. While we often see discipline in physical terms, Proverbs shows us its intention to correct, train, and nurture godly character, and emphasises the reason behind it: love.

Love is shown in careful and caring discipline. It is a characteristic of God not to leave us as we are, but to discipline us—because He loves us (see 3:11–12).

In Hebrews 12:7–11, the writer likens God's discipline of His sons to that of a human father. Our fathers' discipline lasts only a few years and may be imperfect, but God's discipline is lifelong and leads to holiness and Christlikeness. If we accept discipline from our earthly fathers, how much more so should we accept it from God!

Just as the wise would readily accept careful discipline, so we should be ready to discipline our children. But why do children need discipline?

Because of original sin, the life of every child has a bias towards folly (Proverbs 22:15). Involved, caring discipline (the rod) is thus needed to get rid of this folly (see also 19:18; 29:15, 17)

The "rod" in Proverbs 13:24 implies physical discipline. Today, we have a proper sensitivity to the use of corporal punishment, but remember, withholding the right discipline will not help the child (v. 18).

Proverbs 13 contains more wise advice to teach our children, such as to speak wisely and truthfully (vv. 3, 5, 17), to be diligent (vv. 4, 11), and to avoid bad company (v. 20). Ephesians 6:4 reminds fathers not to frustrate their children, perhaps by having inconsistent or unreasonably high standards. Rather, they are to nurture and train children in the way of the Lord, and be examples of godliness to their children.

Discipline that is motivated by love, insightful, and appropriate for the emotional make-up of each child—this is the pattern of child-raising that is endorsed by Scripture.

How can you apply God's discipline and correction in the lives of your children in the way taught by Scripture?

Are you a nurturing, godly influence to your children or the young ones in your life?

Day 23

Read Proverbs 14

A picture is often said to be worth a thousand words—just right for the human mind, which author William Macneile Dixon described as more of a picture gallery than a debating hall. The book of Proverbs works in the picture galleries of our minds, offering short, catchy sayings that make an impact and are memorable.

Notice the use of visual metaphors in Proverbs 14:

- The erection and demolition of a house (v. 1). This is a familiar picture: wisdom builds, but folly demolishes. One leads to security, the other to devastation. The house represents one's family, which can be strengthened or weakened.

- Lashing versus protection (v. 3). Foolish talk hurts the speaker, making him his own worst enemy, while wise, discreet words protect.

- A barn devoid of oxen—and harvest (v. 4). The absence of oxen means that ploughing is not being done. A productive life may be messy, but it leads to growth and results. Investing in oxen comes at a cost, but it reaps benefits.

- A house versus a tent (v. 11). A house may seem more solid and secure than a tent, but wisdom builds up while wickedness destroys.

That which is built by a righteous person will blossom like a tree, bringing forth new life because of his uprightness.

- An inheritance to be avoided (v. 18). An inheritance should sustain life, but the gullible and simple will only get folly, which will destroy their lives. The prudent, on the other hand, will inherit the riches of knowledge.

- A crown (v. 24). This proverb, which concludes the section on wealth and poverty (vv. 20–24), notes the blessing of material benefits upon those who are wise because of their diligence (v. 23). In contrast, folly pays a dividend—more folly.

- A fortress and a refuge (v. 26). The Lord gives the greatest security to those who fear Him, and their families.

- The life-giving fountain and a deadly snare (v. 27; see also 13:14). Reverence for the Lord will deliver us from death and give us life.

- A healthy body versus diseased bones (14:30). A contented life is good for the body, but envy and constant striving is unhealthy.

The attractiveness of following the Lord and His ways can be seen in the various images used in this chapter:

from a house, a crown, and a fortress to a gushing fountain and a healthy body. **Security and satisfaction is elusive unless we turn to the Lord and walk in His ways; only He can give true security and truly satisfy.**

Proverbs 14 reminds us that God's ways and wisdom lead to security, protection, deliverance, a rich harvest, blessing, health, and true life.

ThinkThrough

Which of the images in Proverbs 14 strike you? How can you apply the lessons they illustrate to your life?

The image of a shelter is used in verses 1 and 11. What kind of "house" are you building in your life?

Day 24

Read Proverbs 15

One of the characteristics of God's Word, which tells us all we need to know in order to be saved and to live the Christian life, is its clarity. God is a keen communicator, and He spoke in order to be understood. Under the oversight of His Spirit, the authors of the Bible were keen to communicate clearly as well.

One way they did this was through the creative use of illustrations. Yesterday, we saw in Proverbs 14 a range of illustrations used to teach on wisdom, righteousness, and other topics. In Proverbs 15, we see a number of references to body parts—the tongue (vv. 2, 4), the lips (v. 7), the mouth (vv. 14, 28), the heart (vv. 11, 13–15, 28, 30), and the bones (v. 30).

Today, we shall focus on the ear—its importance is also implied in verses 31–32—and the tongue.

The wise—aware how little they know—listen to correction and take advice (vv. 5, 22, 31, 32). In contrast, the foolish, lacking self-awareness and not recognising their own limitations, refuse to listen (vv. 5, 10, 12, 22, 32). In doing so, these verses warn that they despise themselves and doom themselves to failed plans and destruction.

The deaf ear is matched by a tongue that is harsh (v. 1), destructive (v. 4), foolish (v. 14), and wicked (v. 28).

Proverbs 15 also tells us what the Lord loves and what He hates. He loves the prayer of the upright (v. 8), their pursuit of righteousness (v. 9), and their gracious words (v. 26). He detests the sacrifices of the wicked (v. 8), because they want to get their way with God while holding onto their wickedness. And He detests those who pursue injustice (v. 9).

It is good to remember that God cannot be fooled. He sees everything (v. 3) and knows the inner lives and thoughts of all (v. 11).

At the same time, God is an active participant in the lives of His people. He blesses the upright, but frustrates the lazy (v. 19); He defends the weak, but brings down the proud (v. 25); and He hears the whispered prayers of His own, but stands away from the wicked (v. 29).

God is always everywhere to see, hear, correct, rebuke, and sustain. Reflecting on God's presence, King David noted that even if he fled to the heights or depths, the east or west, "even there your hand will guide me, your right hand will hold me fast" (Psalm 139:10). Dutch theologian Herman Bavinck once said: "There is no place where you may flee. Will you flee from Him? Flee to Him."[5]

[5] Herman Bavinck, *Doctrine of God*, trans. William Hendriksen (Edinburgh: Banner of Truth Trust, 1996)

How can you make sure you have a listening ear and a pure tongue?

How are you encouraged by the assurance of God's continual presence?

Day 25

Read Proverbs 15

Many of us see the heart as the centre of our emotions, so we talk of "loving with all your heart". In the time of Proverbs, the heart represented the centre of the whole person—the conscience, will, emotions, and mind. Hence, when urging Israel to remember what God had done, Moses told them never to "let them fade from your heart" (Deuteronomy 4:9).

Today, we look at the references to the heart in Proverbs 15 (vv. 7, 11, 13–15, 28, 30).

The two types of heart—the righteous and the wicked—are contrasted by the words they produce on the lips and mouth (vv. 7, 28). The righteous heart speaks gently and wisely, and seeks to soothe and edify. In contrast, the wicked heart frustrates, spreads ignorance, and discourages (vv. 1, 2, 4, 28).

Verses 13–15 describe the happy and cheerful heart. It is evidenced by a person's face, just as a sorrowful heart is seen in a crushed spirit (v. 13); it zealously seeks additional knowledge (v. 14); and it remains cheerful despite the wretched circumstances of life (v. 16; see also 14:30). This description suggests that true happiness and joy come from the heart, and depend more on the inner being of a person than on his circumstances.

Christians are never so impressive as when they remain hopeful and steadfast amid crisis and catastrophe. In the face of pain, failure, and loss, can a person still say as Job did: "The LORD gave and the LORD has taken away; may the name of the LORD be praised" (Job 1:21)?

These verses tell us the relationship between the internal (the heart and the spirit) and the external (the face and body language, and circumstances of life):

• The state of the heart can affect the face, body language, and spirit (Proverbs 15:13).

• The circumstances of life may not necessarily affect the heart and the spirit (v. 15; see also Philippians 4:12–13). The key to remaining steadfast and content in any situation is to seek knowledge (Proverbs 15:14); such a discerning heart listens to God's revelation and finds its conviction there, and therefore, is able to view all circumstances through the lens of His Word.

In contrast, the fool has no stable foundation to deal with the changing circumstances of life.

How firm a foundation, you saints of the Lord,
is laid for your faith in His excellent word!
What more can He say than to you He has said,
who unto the Saviour, for refuge have fled.
—Richard Keene

What do your words, general disposition, and outlook in life reveal about your heart?

The key to a cheerful heart is discernment. How are you seeking discernment from God's Word? How can you seek His knowledge?

Day 26

Read Proverbs 16

The Bible was divided into chapters in the 13th century, and into verses in the 16th century. Most of the chapters in Proverbs contain about 25 to 35 verses, and sometimes the opening verse is indicative of the chapter's general theme.

Proverbs 16 is one such chapter. The first and last verses (vv. 1, 33) have the same theme: the sovereignty of God.

Unlike animals which are driven by instinct, human beings have the ability and reasoning to make plans (vv. 1, 9). **But it is the Lord, who knows the motive behind our plans, and who determines their outcome** (vv. 1–2); our plans will come through only if God allows it. God's oversight is further emphasised in verse 4: "The LORD works out everything to its proper end", reminding us that it is wise to commit our plans to Him (v. 3).

In Old Testament times, God's people often used the "lot" (v. 33) to discern God's guidance. Small stones were cast, and the result was considered to be an answer from the Lord. To the people of Israel, it was God—and not chance—who ruled in all things. With the coming of the Holy Spirit at Pentecost, however, casting of the lot was no longer seen as necessary; it was last used to choose Matthias to replace Judas in Acts 1:26.

In Proverbs 16:10–15, Solomon continues on the subject of rule, but now speaks of earthly kings.

As the king of Israel, Solomon knew that kings were meant to be representatives of God, and their words were thus authoritative (v. 10). Kings therefore must not betray justice, but establish righteousness and honesty (vv. 12–13). As they have the ability to bring happiness or misery to their people (vv. 14–15), they have great responsibility. They should stand against the scoundrel (v. 27), the perverse (v. 28), the violent (v. 29), and the schemer (v. 30).

How happy Israel must have been to have such a wise king in Solomon! Unfortunately, the best of men are, ultimately, men at best. Solomon's downfall came through his love of foreign women, showing that those who rule are subject to extraordinary temptation.

We may complain and criticise those in power, but do we pray for them? We need to pray regularly for those who rule us (see 1 Timothy 2:1–2). Pray for justice to be done through them

(Proverbs 16:10); for them to be humble (v. 18), which can be difficult for those in exalted positions; and for them to recognise that the Lord reigns, even over kings (vv. 1, 33).

ThinkThrough

Earthly rulers are God's servants (Romans 13:4, 6). Have you been praying for them? Commit them to the Lord in prayer today.

According to theologian John Calvin, the most important truth is "that God governs the whole world by His care". What evidence can you see of this truth each day? What plans do you need to submit to God's providential care today?

Day 27

Read Proverbs 15:16–17; 16:8–19

Comparison is a common literary device in Proverbs; the writers use it to stress the value of an object or quality by comparing it with another. They often compare material and spiritual wealth, or internal and external values, showing that one is far more valuable than the other. Let's take another look at several "Better . . . than . . ." examples in Proverbs 15 and 16.

More wealth is usually seen as better than less, but not if it means neglecting to acknowledge the Lord and His sovereignty in our lives (15:16). Not doing so will only lead to turmoil. Reverence for the Lord is more important than material gain.

It is better to have less to eat (a simple meal of vegetables) but enjoy loving relationships, than to have a feast of meat but have no love in one's life (15:17). This comparison stresses the value of relationships and contentment over material wealth.

Again, it is better to have less if it comes with righteousness, rather than more if the gain comes as a result of injustice (16:8).

Wisdom and good judgment are better than gold and silver, which the world values (16:16). This is a central truth emphasised in Proverbs. Wealth cannot buy wisdom, and must never be gained at the expense of wisdom. Riches are not necessarily bad, but not when it results in pride (16:19). It is better to be poor and to be counted with the oppressed than to be proud.

These comparisons stress the ultimate importance of fear of the Lord, relationships, inner satisfaction, righteousness, wisdom, and humility. **Believers are reminded to seek these values first—even if it means giving up the benefits of wealth and status, which the world places great value.**

Followers of Jesus will never regret the decision to follow Him, for they will be rewarded either in this life or the next. Not only is the Lord Jesus better than any alternative, but He is the best. He has "become for us wisdom from God—that is, our righteousness, holiness and redemption" (1 Corinthians 1:30). May we say as Peter did: "Lord, to whom shall we go? You have the words of eternal life" (John 6:68).

ThinkThrough

How has God blessed you in areas other than material wealth? Spend some time thanking Him today.

Think about the times when you have had to choose between material wealth and reverence for the Lord, righteousness, justice, or wisdom. How did you respond? How can the comparisons of Proverbs 15 and 16 guide you?

Day 28

Read Proverbs 17

Proverbs 17 continues to offer advice on seeking wisdom and directions on how to live in a way that pleases God. This chapter includes more mentions of the tongue, the ear, money, friendships, justice, reward, and discernment. Let's look at a few of the proverbs focusing on godly actions and attitudes.

The value of wisdom: The wise and discerning will ultimately receive more honour than the reckless son, even though they may be a servant (v. 2). This comparison was especially significant in those times, when servants rarely progressed beyond their station in life. This proverb shows that wisdom and ability are better than inherited privilege, which can be forfeited. Solomon himself recognised the value of one of his officials, Jeroboam, and promoted him; in the end, Jeroboam would rise to prominence over Solomon's own son Rehoboam (1 Kings 11:28–31).

How God purifies: Just as fire refines gold and silver by removing the impurities, the Lord purifies His people, improving and developing their character by allowing difficulties to take place in their lives (Proverbs 17:3). **How often we can testify that times of pain and testing were also times of growth and advancement in our godliness!** God uses such times to bring grace into our lives.

The sin of bribery: A bribe is thought to be effective by the one who gives it; it may actually open doors (v. 8). But does God approve of bribery? Verses 15 and 23 make it plain that corruption works against justice, and is detested by God. Both the person who gives the bribe and the one who receives it are acting against God's will.

The danger of quarrels: Like a small hole in the dam that leads to disaster, a quarrel may be a little thing, but once started is hard to control, and may develop into a long term feud (v. 14). This proverb advises restraint in an argument, noting that it is better to "drop the matter" than to risk turning it into a full-blown dispute. Beware arguing over a minor issue—a little leak can collapse a dam!

Verse 19 gives another warning on quarrelling, comparing those who love a quarrel to those who build a high gate. The common element here is arrogance. Those who love disputes are often full of pride, just like those who build a high gate to show off their wealth. Both also believe they will remain safe behind their arguments and their tall defences. But verse 19 makes clear that such arrogance will result in catastrophe.

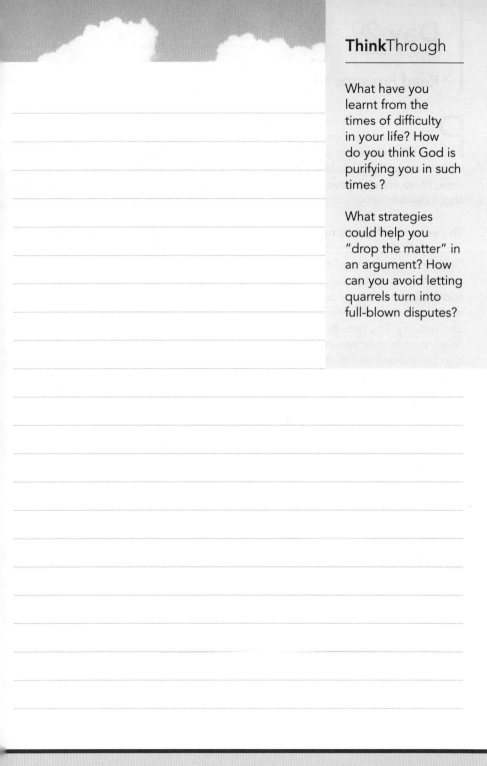

ThinkThrough

What have you learnt from the times of difficulty in your life? How do you think God is purifying you in such times ?

What strategies could help you "drop the matter" in an argument? How can you avoid letting quarrels turn into full-blown disputes?

Day 29

Read Proverbs 18

Proverbs 18 offers several notable observations about God, our speech, marriage, and friendship. In contrast to the people we should seek, there are also several types we should avoid.

The security of God's name: Verses 10–11 compare the name of God with the wealth of the rich. God's name means His person, character, and attributes; the righteous who depend on Him will find true safety and security. The rich, on the other hand, trust in their wealth, imagining it to be unassailable. But this is a false sense of security, as we have seen in previous comparisons of wealth and righteousness.

Watching one's words: Two complementary observations are made about the tongue. Verses 6–7 describe how a fool talks himself into trouble, while verses 20–21 note how a wise person's speech benefits him. Together, they warn us to be careful with our speech, for the tongue has great potential for good or ill—"the power of life and death" (v. 21). **When thinking about whether one should speak, the old maxim, "When in doubt, don't", is worth remembering.**

Marriage: Finding a wife is a good thing, according to verse 22. It will involve effort and searching, but it is worth it! This proverb can be seen in the light of God's gift of a helpmate to Adam (Genesis 2:18–20), when God noted that "it is not good for the man to be alone".

Friendship: Fair-weather friends are of no use to a man, compared to those who stick by him through thick and thin (Proverbs 18:24). This proverb puts together the warning of 19:4—"wealth attracts many friends"—and the encouraging advice of 17:17, "A friend loves at all times, and a brother is born for a time of adversity." A true friend is constant and loyal; it is a boon to have one and to be one.

This chapter of Proverbs also talks about several types of people we should avoid:

- The unfriendly man, whose sole area of interest is himself (18:1). Such a man never asks for advice and wants only to do things his own way; not surprisingly, he is likely to start quarrels.

- The fool, who like the unfriendly man, also has no interest in receiving knowledge; he is only interested in airing his own opinion (v. 2). Such a man, notes Derek Kidner in his commentary on Proverbs, has a "closed mind" but "open mouth".[6]

- The gossip, whose words are tantalising (v. 8). These "choice morsels" are savoured and digested, and will likely be well remembered— even though they may be based on hearsay.

- The slacker, who harms himself and society either through his lack of productivity or his sloppy and careless work (v. 9). Here he is being compared to the man who destroys; both their works have similar effect.

- The person who is offended—whether a relative or friend—with whom it is very difficult to restore former intimacies (v. 19). In noting that trying to win him back is like trying to conquer a well-defended city, this proverb is stressing the impact of serious disputes.

[6] Kidner, *Proverbs* (2009), 127

Take another look at the type of people to avoid. Do you fit into any of the categories? How can you be "a friend who sticks closer than a brother" (Proverbs 18:24)?

Proverbs 18:10 offers an encouraging promise to those who "run to" the Lord. What does it mean to seek refuge in the Lord, in practical terms?

Day 30

Read Proverbs 19

We have been warned that "bad company corrupts good character" (1 Corinthians 15:33). So what are the kinds of "bad company" that we should avoid? And what are the types of good company should we keep instead? We saw some examples of bad company in Proverbs 18. Proverbs 19 gives more examples of people we should avoid, along with those whose company we should keep instead.

Whose company should we avoid?

- **The fool (v. 1).** Such a man despises godly, righteous speech, and indulges in twisted speech that seeks to deceive or cause trouble. He may also be like the man who rages against the Lord and blames Him for all his troubles (v. 3).

- **The false witness (vv. 5, 9, 28),** who denies people justice by lying in court. He will not escape punishment.

- **The sluggard (v. 15).** Lack of activity and lethargy causes such a man to fall in deep sleep instead of working hard to provide for himself. As a result, he is unable to feed himself.

- **The mocker (v. 25),** who has a closed mind and refuses correction. The simple may learn from watching the mocker being punished, while the discerning will learn from just a rebuke. Punishment is also in store for the mocker (v. 29).

Whose company should we keep?

- **The wise (v. 8),** who cherishes wisdom and understanding. Such a person listens to advice (vv. 20, 27) and learns from rebuke (v. 25).

- **The kind (v. 17),** who makes an eternal investment when he helps the poor.

- **The patient (v. 11),** who is neither hasty in his decisions (v. 2) nor hot-tempered in his responses (v. 19). Slow to anger, he is also willing to overlook an offence (v. 11).

- **The blameless (v. 1),** who knows it is better to live a life of integrity even if it means being poor, than to be wealthy and live outside of God's will and ways.

The key conviction which drives these traits is the fear of the Lord (v. 23). It is the core of all wisdom and the greatest of all virtues. Every characteristic to be embraced flows from this one fear.

Reverence for God leads to life and brings about deep contentment, enabling us to remain unruffled by the changing circumstances of life—so that "one rests content, untouched by trouble" (v. 23). Many years after Proverbs was written, Jesus would come along and personally offer this same assurance of contentment that comes from following Him: "Peace I leave with you; my peace I give you. I do not give to you as the world gives. Do not let your hearts be troubled and do not be afraid" (John 14:27).

Who would be the "bad company" to avoid in your life? Who would be the "good company" to keep?

How would the qualities of both bad and good company apply to you? Are you good or bad company to others?

Day 31

Read Proverbs 20

Some people may be surprised to find a book like Proverbs in the Bible, given that it contains so much common-sense advice—not unlike a collection of wise sayings they might find in a secular book. But we shouldn't be surprised. **After all, good common sense comes from God, and it is available to all who are willing to listen and learn.** Proverbs 20 is one of the many examples of chapters in the book that contain good common sense.

- Drunkenness leads to aggressive behaviour and poor judgment (v. 1). It is not wise to be under the influence of wine and beer, as they can lead to wrongful behaviour (31:4–7).

- The fool is quick to be offended and get into a fight, which just makes matters worse (20:3). Cool it!

- Many claim to be a faithful friend, but talk is cheap (v. 6). True friendship will be tested by times of difficulty.

- Knowing oneself—and one's sinful self—well is an important aspect of wisdom (v. 9). "Who can say, 'I have kept my heart pure?'" is a rhetorical question, for no one is perfect (Romans 3:10). No one has a right to moral superiority, and we are to resist judgmentalism and self-righteousness.

- Beware the shrewdness of buyers, who haggle for a lower price by claiming the item is worthless— only to brag about the bargain later (Proverbs 20:14)! Wisdom allows us to discern between truth and deception in people's words.

- Things obtained by dishonest means or deception are appealing and may bring momentary satisfaction (v. 17), but ultimately they will be unsatisfying and possibly even destructive, like how gravel destroys the teeth.

- Don't be impulsive or arrogant; seek advice before making and carrying out any plans (v. 18; see also 11:14, 15:22). Jesus, when speaking of counting the cost, also highlighted the value of seeking wise counsel before waging war (Luke 14:31).

- Gaining an inheritance "too soon" implies obtaining it by unjust or unrighteous means (Proverbs 20:21)—an act that will ultimately not end well, perhaps because of divine justice.

- The old and young have their unique, respective strengths (v. 29); this observation is a reminder for the young and old to respect and appreciate each other.

The problem with common sense is

that it is not so common. That is why Proverbs is such a precious book. It is, as Bible commentator Matthew Henry put it: "A complete body of divine ethics . . . exposing every vice, recommending every virtue, and suggesting rules for the government of ourselves in every relation and condition and every turn of the conversation."

ThinkThrough

Which of the "common-sense" advice in Proverbs 20 strikes you most? Why? How can you apply it to your life?

Proverbs 20:12 notes that God gave us ears to hear (wise counsel and teaching) and eyes to discern (what is right and wrong). How can we keep our eyes and ears open to assess other "common-sense" advice we hear in the light of His Word?

Day 32

Read Proverbs 21

Solomon's exceptional, God-given wisdom is described in 1 Kings 3 and 4. Such was his reputation that "from all nations people came to listen to Solomon's wisdom, sent by all the kings of the world, who had heard of his wisdom" (1 Kings 4:34). It is not strange, therefore, that Solomon should speak of kings and rulers in the proverbs he penned.

Proverbs 21:1 is one such example. In Solomon's day, kings possessed absolute authority and believed that they had the power to make decisions on their own. But this proverb is a clear reminder that the Lord is sovereign and rules over all things— the Lord is the King of kings!

All kings are God's servants (see Romans 13:1–2)—even those who do not acknowledge Him. They are all under His rule and control (see what Isaiah 41:2–4 and 45:13 say about God's use of Cyrus the Persian king).

Proverbs 21 ends with yet another reminder (vv. 30–31) that no-one can frustrate the purposes of God. No plan or wisdom can succeed if it goes against God or His will (v. 30), and no military campaign, however well planned, can be victorious unless the Lord allows it (v. 31).

Like Proverbs 1:7 ("The fear of the LORD is the beginning of knowledge"),

21:30 ("There is no wisdom, no insight, no plan that can succeed against the LORD") is a key verse in the book of Proverbs. **Both point to the same truth—God is sovereign and is to be revered**. This truth should drive all our thought, actions, words, and attitudes, and it lies behind the teachings found in the rest of Proverbs 21:

- The Lord searches even hidden motives (vv. 2–4). He cannot be deceived, for He knows men's hearts. He looks for true integrity, and can see any sign of arrogance within.

- There is nothing inherently wrong with wealth, but it must not be gained at the expense of integrity (v. 6). In everything you do, remember that the end does not justify the means; reject the "whatever it takes" approach.

- Do not forsake the path of wisdom and godly living, or you will end up suffering the punishment for sin—death (v. 16).

- Plan for the future and live wisely, don't live just for the present (v. 20). This proverb compares the wise person who stores up food with the fool who eats up everything he has and has nothing to spare.

- Pursue righteousness and love (v. 21), for they will bring their own rewards of life, prosperity, and honour. This means leading a life that is pleasing to God and a blessing to others.

- Beware the ever-present temptation of overweening pride (v. 24). To reject rebuke, to turn a deaf ear to good advice, and to mock those who rebuke and advise you is to give in to pride.

ThinkThrough

How does knowing God's absolute sovereignty over everything we do affect how you live every day? How will it affect the plans you make in your life?

Reflect on what Proverbs 21:2–4 says about how God knows and sees all. What would He see in your heart and your motivations? Would they please Him?

Day 33

Read Proverbs 22:1–16

The book of Job shows what happens when a formula is applied rigidly and insensitively to life. According to Job's friends, he must have been suffering because he had sinned. This was based on the supposed principle that sin always leads to punishment and righteousness to blessing.

But life does not always work according to a fixed formula. In Psalm 73:1–14, the psalmist notes that the rich get away with their sin and pride, while he suffers afflictions despite having kept his heart pure. In Job 42:7, we also see God rebuking Job's friends for having misrepresented Him.

In the same way, proverbs are not rigid formulas, laws, or iron-clad promises; rather, they are divinely inspired observations and generalisations about life.

Proverbs 22:6 is one such example. It observes that starting a child on good principles with proper instruction and discipline will generally produce adults who continue on the wise path. Responsible parenting should bear fruit in responsible, mature offspring. However, this is not a solid promise; rather, it is an observation that encourages good parenting. It should not be misused and taken to mean that a child who does not turn out well indicates deficient parenting, or that a child who turns out well is entirely the result of good parenting.

Other proverbs in this chapter contain similar general observations about life:

- Walking humbly in reverence to God is generally conducive to gaining an honourable reputation and wealth (v. 4). Of course, it doesn't mean humble people will always be rich and honoured.

- To guard our soul, we need to keep to the path of wisdom, avoid the company of the wicked, and resist their influence, for they will take us down a path filled with snares and pitfalls (v. 5). This would generally preserve us from such dangers—but it doesn't mean that we still won't face difficulties along our way.

- You will reap what you sow (v. 8). Though we may not see evidence of this truth on this earth, it will be ultimately proven in the light of eternity. This is something Asaph, the writer of Psalm 73, discovered after some reflection. After wondering why the wicked seemed to do so well, he saw their "final destiny", in which God would "place them on slippery ground" and "cast them down to ruin" (Psalm 73:17–18).

- Generosity leads to blessing for all involved, including the giver and the recipient (Proverbs 22:9). But this principle should not encourage greed, giving in order to receive!

Verse 15 gives another proverb on child-rearing. The first line gives the diagnosis: folly comes naturally to the child—after all, we are all born sinners. The second line provides the prescription: involved, intentional discipline and instruction will get rid of this folly. Parental guidance is important, for children who are left to themselves will generally not turn out well.

A Christian mother, when asked what she did with her time, replied, "I am a builder." She was then asked, "What do you build?" Her answer: "I build character!"

What is your personal experience with the observations in Proverbs 22 about the results of walking humbly, avoiding bad company, and being generous? How would you interpret these proverbs in the light of today's insights and your own experience?

Reflect on your own motivations for doing some of these things (e.g. being generous). How are you encouraged by Proverbs 22?

Day 34

Read Proverbs 22:17–24:22

The "Thirty sayings of the wise", were not written by Solomon himself, and scholars are divided over their source. Because of some similarity to an ancient Egyptian work, some believe that Solomon adapted them, but others differ.

What's important is that they are still from God. The Bible is the inspired Word of God. **No matter which human hands wrote the words, they say precisely what God wants to say, therefore we are to listen, learn, and apply them to our lives** (Proverbs 22:17). Let's take a quick look at these 30 sayings, before we go into greater detail about some of them tomorrow:

1. Keep these sayings in your heart and apply them, so that you will trust in the Lord. (22:17–21)

2. Don't exploit the poor, for the Lord is their protector. (vv. 22–23)

3. Watch whom you associate with, for you may follow their ways. (vv. 24–25)

4. Be prudent in your financial commitments. (vv. 26–27)

5. Do not appropriate other people's property. (v. 28)

6. The quality of your work will determine your progress. (v. 29)

7. Beware the temptation of gluttony, for it can trap you. (23:1–3)

8. Don't pursue wealth, for the security of riches is fleeting. (vv. 4–5)

9. Don't accept an invitation from a stingy host, the meal will not be enjoyable. (vv. 6–8)

10. Don't waste your effort advising fools, it will be like casting a pearl before swine. (v. 9)

11. Don't take property from orphans, the Lord is their defender. (vv. 10–11)

12. Listen to wisdom, keep it in your heart, and apply it. (v. 12)

13. Proper discipline will benefit a child. (vv. 13–14)

14. A wise and righteous child is a father's joy. (vv. 15–16)

15. Don't envy the prosperity of the wicked, but focus on revering the Lord, for it will give you true hope. (vv.17–18)

16. Don't associate with those who indulge in drinking and feasting, for their partying will only lead them into poverty. (vv. 19–21)

17. Heed the wisdom and advice of your parents, and you will be their joy. (vv. 22–25)

18. Beware the woman who seduces you into unfaithfulness, for she will lead you into a trap. (vv. 26–28)

19. Don't indulge in drinking, it will bring all kinds of trouble. (vv. 29–35)

20. Don't envy the wicked, for they are always plotting trouble. (24:1–2)

21. Wisdom is the key to a stable house and to success. (vv. 3–4)

22. Wisdom gives true strength; good guidance and advice are needed for victory. (vv. 5–6)

23. Wisdom is out of a fool's reach, so he should keep quiet when decisions are being made. (v. 7)

24. Evil plots and foolish schemes are sin. (vv. 8–9)

25. Persevere through trouble, and help others. Don't claim ignorance of their predicament, for the Lord knows what's in your heart. (vv. 10–12)

26. Wisdom will give you true joy and hope. (vv. 13–14)

27. Don't attack or rob the righteous, for they are protected. (vv. 15–16)

28. Don't gloat over others' misfortunes, even if they are your enemy or are unrighteous, for it displeases the Lord. (vv. 17–18)

29. Don't fret about the success of the wicked, they will be punished in due course. (vv. 19–20)

30. Fear God and those He puts in authority, do not rebel against them. (vv. 21–22)

These lessons might seem random, but life, after all, is typically random too. Who knows—you might find one especially apt today. Consider taking time to reflect on the 30 sayings over the next 30 days, and see how you can apply them to your life.

Which of the 30 sayings of the wise strike you most? How can you apply them to your daily life?

What do the 30 wise sayings say about the nature and character of our Lord? How can this knowledge encourage you and influence the way you live?

Read Proverbs 22:17–24:22

The atheist philosopher Bertrand Russell once observed that most people would rather die than think—and that most people do!

Today, let's look at 4 of the 30 sayings of the wise, starting with the introduction in Proverbs 22:17–21, which contains the appeal to listen carefully, to keep the 30 wise teachings in our hearts and on our lips, and to apply them (vv. 17–18). This means paying close attention to them, taking time to reflect on them, and thinking about how we can share and apply them.

This takes intentional effort. The wisdom contained in these 30 sayings is not to be stored away, but applied in our own lives as well as shared with others to encourage them (vv. 17–18), with the aim of growing our trust in the Lord (v. 19). As we meditate on these wise sayings, it will lead to sound and truthful speech (v. 21).

Saying 5 (22:28): During the time of Solomon, the limits of people's property were often marked by boundary stones. Moving these stones amounted to stealing property, since a person would effectively increase his property and reduce that of his neighbour. This could have a great impact on people's lives, because land was a source of livelihood and security to farmers (see Job 24:2), as well as an inheritance to be passed on to the next generation. Stealing property was considered a sin against God because land in Israel was owned and apportioned by Him (see Deuteronomy 19:14).

Saying 15 (23:17–18): Sometimes the wicked seem to be successful in life, which can make us envious or prompt us to question the justice of it all, as the writer of Psalm 73, Asaph, did. But the Bible reminds us that the wicked are ultimately like chaff (Psalm 1:4); what they accumulate are only trifles. **We are to take the long-term view, knowing that the eternal security of those who fear the Lord is assured** (Proverbs 23:18). How much better it is to revere God and be assured of a future!

Saying 17 (23:22–25): Without our parents, we would not have life. They have our best interests at heart, we are not to despise their advice and instruction (v. 22). Instead, we are to prize and hold on to truth and wisdom (v. 23) so that we will be wise and righteous, and thus bring joy and delight to our parents (v. 24). The fifth of the Ten Commandments directs us to honour our parents (Exodus 20:12), and Proverbs encourages it by showing us the joys and blessings that a wise child brings to his parents.

Saying 27 (24:15–16): It is futile to raid or rob the righteous, because they will not allow any setback to keep them down and will rise again (v. 16). They know that evil will never triumph and will ultimately be punished (v. 16). The righteous trust in God, knowing that He is the defender of the righteous, the fatherless (see 23:11), and the poor (22:23), and will therefore act on behalf of those who belong to Him (see 14:31).

> And though they take our life,
> Goods, honour, children, wife,
> Yet is their profit small;
> These things shall vanish all
> The city of God remaineth.
> —Martin Luther

ThinkThrough

What goes through your mind when you see the wicked prosper? How can you draw encouragement from Proverbs 23:17–18? How can you respond in a godly manner?

Proverbs 24:16 notes that the righteous will "rise again" even though they may fall seven times. Why are they able to do so? What would give you strength to rise again even when afflicted?

Day 36

Read Proverbs 24:23–34

Before we return to Solomon's proverbs, we have five more sayings from the "wise" (Proverbs 24:23–34). They are possibly adapted from ancient Egyptian wisdom writing, though scholars remain unsure. The theme running through these sayings is a well-ordered society that promotes justice and truthfulness. These are attributes of God himself and are reflected in His creation, where wisdom ensures order in place of chaos (8:30).

The well-ordered society is one in which:

- The guilty are convicted because there is no partiality in judgment (24:23–25).

- Speech is honest, and is seen as a blessing and kindness (v. 26).

- False testimony and deception are avoided (v. 28).

We live in a society that tolerates the "white lie"—the inconsequential, well-meaning untruth, or a small lie told to save face or avoid embarrassment. But all forms of lying are wrong, and represent a failure to face up to and reflect reality. White lies, or "spin", as psychologist Jordan B. Peterson puts it in his book, *12 Rules to Life: An Antidote to Chaos*, is "the speech people engage in when they attempt to influence and manipulate others". **We are to strive for honesty and truthfulness. Lying and deceptive speech is the Serpent's heart language and is to be avoided.**

Proverbs 24:30–34 is a close parallel to 6:6–11, which makes the same observation about laziness and contrasts the sluggard with the industrious ant. In 24:30–34, the sluggard neglects his vineyard and wall (v. 31) because he would rather rest and sleep; his life is not grounded in the reality that laziness will only lead to poverty. Theologian John Calvin said that three vices prevail much, even among pastors—"sloth, desire of gain, and lust for power".[7]

Sloth comes naturally to us and must be resisted by meaningful, productive work. Be like the ant who contributes to the needs of its community.

[7] John Calvin, *Bible Commentaries On The Catholic Epistles* (Germany: Jazzybee Verlag, 2012), 92.

ThinkThrough

In what situations might you be tempted to tell a white lie? What practical steps can you take to avoid this temptation?

How might the warning of Proverbs 24:33–34 apply in modern life? How can we balance the need for proper rest and the warning against laziness?

Day 37

Read Proverbs 25

After the death of Solomon, the nation of Israel was divided into two kingdoms—the northern kingdom of Israel, which consisted of 10 of the 12 tribes; and the southern kingdom of Judah, which was made up of the other 2 tribes, Benjamin and Judah.

Hezekiah, a descendant of David, was the 13th king of Judah. During his reign, the Assyrians had conquered Israel and were bent on defeating Judah. Hezekiah, who was a godly king, "trusted in the LORD, the God of Israel" and kept His commands (2 Kings 18:5). Subsequently, God delivered Judah from the Assyrians. Concerned with preserving the precious law and wisdom of God for future generations, Hezekiah had scribes compile some 100 of Solomon's proverbs in Proverbs 25 to 29. This was done in a time of insecurity and threat.

Proverbs 25:2–3 reminds the reader of the place of God and the king. **Humankind does not know everything, but God does, and He reveals to us what we need to know.** The king in Israel represents God, but there will still be matters unknown to him. There is always something of mystery about life, and sometimes the king's heart and decisions may not be understood. At such a time, we can only trust in

God, who knows all things and who appoints kings to rule in His name.

Proverbs 25 contains several noteworthy comparisons and words of wisdom:

- Better to start out humbly than to exaggerate your importance—and be humiliated (vv. 6–7; see also Luke 14:7–11).

- The right ruling and wise rebuke are as precious as gold, silver, and beautiful ornaments (Proverbs 25:11–12).

- A messenger who is reliable is refreshing to his employer, like a nice cold drink given at a time of hard work (v. 13).

- An empty promise is like weather that seems to promise much rain, but delivers none (v. 14).

- Honey is sweet and pleasant to eat, but too much of a good thing has unpleasant consequences (vv. 16, 27). Avoid excesses and extremes, it is wise to seek moderation.

- A lie or false testimony is as damaging and hurtful as a sword that pierces the flesh or a club that bludgeons (v. 18).

- Be aware of whom you trust (v. 19). Relying on unfaithful friends in troubled times is like depending on a broken tooth when eating or on a lame foot when running—they are not only useless, but also painful.

- Trying to bring cheer to someone who's depressed with a happy song is insensitive and will hurt even more—like pouring stinging vinegar on a wound or taking away a jacket when it's cold (v. 20).

- Peace in a marriage is more important than the physical comfort of a house (v. 24; see also 21:9, 19). It is better to live on a roof or in the desert—exposed to the elements—than to live inside with a quarrelsome spouse.

- News in those days may not have travelled fast, but when good news finally reached its hearers, it gave life and revived a weary soul (25:25).

- A person who compromises his integrity pollutes himself (v. 26). Keep yourself pure and resist wickedness!

- Lack of self-control and restraint leaves a person exposed to danger (v. 28).

ThinkThrough

King Hezekiah treasured God's law and wisdom greatly, and did what he could to preserve them in people's hearts. How much do you value God's wisdom? What practical steps can you take to keep them in your mind and heart?

Which of Solomon's proverbs in chapter 25 strike you most? How can you apply his wisdom to your own life?

Day 38

Read Proverbs 26

There are three major characters in Proverbs 26: the fool (vv. 1–12), the sluggard (vv. 13–16), and the troublemaker (vv. 17–28).

The fool (vv. 1–12) is the person out of touch with reality. He does not recognise his own need, and wants no one's advice, for he thinks he knows it all (v. 12). He is proud and has an inflated view of himself. We are told not to honour a fool (vv. 1, 8), reason with him (vv. 4, 5), trust him (vv. 6, 10), listen to him (vv. 7, 9), or rely on him (v. 10). Like a horse and a donkey, a fool can only be guided by brute force (v. 3). **Don't be unteachable like the fool!**

The sluggard (vv. 13–16) has made his bed his home, and gives the excuse that it's too dangerous to leave the house (v. 13). Anchored to his bed, he tosses in it and doesn't get up, like a door secured to its hinge (v. 14)—he and his bed are inseparable. Like the fool, the sluggard is also self-deluded and thinks he has no need for wise advice (v. 16). He is not only lazy, but also proud.

The troublemaker (vv. 17–28) may be charming (v. 25), but he is deceptive (v. 24) and cannot keep himself from meddling in matters which have nothing to do with him (v. 17). His mouth is his big problem: he gossips (v. 20), starts quarrels (v. 21), professes love while concealing hatred and malice (vv. 23–26), and lies (v. 28).

A person's words can reveal the condition of his heart. But the words of a troublemaker are deceptive, and conceal what lies beneath (v. 23). Though the gossips he tells are choice morsels and go down well (v. 22), they are deadly arrows that kill (v. 18).

These three characters in Proverbs 26 are a stark contrast to the wise person whom we've read about over the past days. Such a person knows himself and his own limitations; he seeks righteousness, lives humbly, fulfils his responsibilities, works diligently, ensures that his words work for peace, and listens to wise advice.

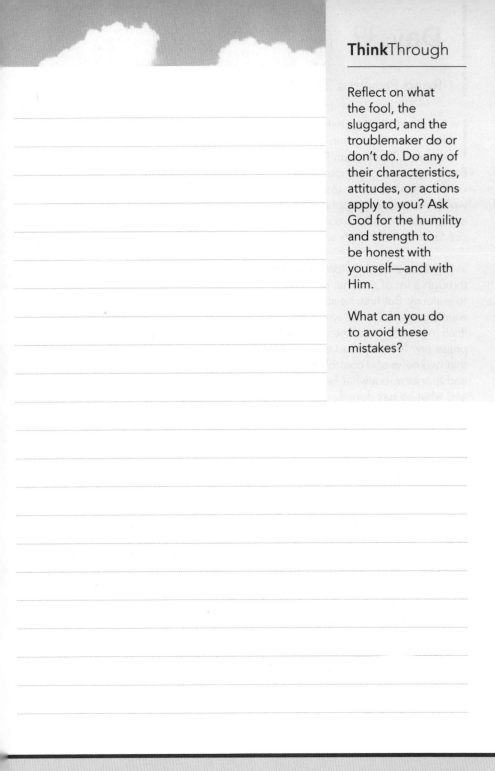

ThinkThrough

Reflect on what the fool, the sluggard, and the troublemaker do or don't do. Do any of their characteristics, attitudes, or actions apply to you? Ask God for the humility and strength to be honest with yourself—and with Him.

What can you do to avoid these mistakes?

Day 39

Read Proverbs 27:1–4

In his play *Othello*, Shakespeare called envy "the green-eyed monster". The Puritan Richard Baxter also warned about envying God's gifts in others—that a man would rather the gospel not be shared and people remain unconverted, than see God work through someone else.

In Proverbs 27:1–4, Solomon moves through a list of sins that build up to jealousy. But first, he starts with a warning against pride, which shows itself in presumptuousness and self-praise (vv. 1–2). A proud man believes that he knows and controls the future, and boasts about what he will do (v. 1) and what he has done (v. 2).

Solomon also warns against overreacting to insulting words from a fool, comparing them to stone and sand, which are heavy, cumbersome, and difficult to handle and transport (v. 3). The comparison captures the unbearable nature of a fool's provocation, which can cause resentment and tempt one to respond in anger. This observation brings us to the next warning against anger (v. 4). **Resentment and anger are bad enough, but jealousy—that brooding covetousness of others' abilities and possessions—is worse than both.**

While anger is cruel (in that it can be destructive) and fury is overwhelming (in that it can be uncontrollable), jealousy is both. Jealousy, which rejoices in others' failure and grieves at their success, destroys both giver and recipient. It poisons a person's own thinking and clouds his judgment, and can prompt him to uncontrollable actions. Jealousy led Joseph's brothers to beat him and sell him off as a slave (Genesis 37:8–10, Acts 7:9), and led the Jewish leaders to implicate Jesus and demand His death (Matthew 27:18). Proverbs 14:30 notes that "envy rots the bones". Theologian C. H. Spurgeon said: "The jealous man poisons the banquet and then sits down and joins in eating it."

So why does God describe himself as being jealous (Exodus 20:5)? The Bible draws a distinction between covetous envy (which is jealousy of others) and the jealousy of God (which is an appropriate jealousy for the love and loyalty of His people). God's jealousy is like a man's jealousy for the love of his wife (Numbers 5:11–31).

How can we guard against pride and envy?

- By depending and trusting in God's sovereign rule (Proverbs 27:1),

How can you remind
yourself to rely on
God's sovereignty
and plan—and
not on your own
abilities—each day?

Reflect on times
when you might
have felt envious
of other people's
abilities and
achievements. Ask
God to help you
learn how to be
content.

instead of being presumptuous and believing in
our ability to control our future.

• By listening to honest, unbiased evaluations,
instead of self-praise (v. 2).

• By choosing to be content instead of harbouring
jealousy (v. 4).

Solomon makes his observations of the destructive
and uncontrollable nature of jealousy without
offering a solution. The New Testament tells us to
put off envy like an old set of clothes, as it is part of
the old life (Galatians 5:21; Colossians 3:8–9).
Titus 3:3 also reminds us that having been saved
from our former lifestyle of envy and malice, we are
to devote ourselves to doing good (Titus 3:8).

The antidote to envy is contentment. According to
Paul, it is something we have to learn. Philippians
4:12 describes what contentment—both in times
of plenty and in times of need—looks like: "I know
what it is to be in need, and I know what it is to
have plenty. I have learned the secret of being
content in any and every situation, whether well fed
or hungry, whether living in plenty or in want."

Day 40

Read Proverbs 27:5–27

We can make three observations about today's passage.

One, the observations in Proverbs 27:5–27 are a bit like life itself—random. They contain insights covering a diverse range of subjects: from the value of friendship (vv. 9–10), being prudent (v. 12), and putting up security (v. 13), to the use of appropriate words (v. 14), the dangers of insatiable desires (v. 20), and pastoral concerns (vv. 23–27). No one knows what each day may bring forth (v. 1), so no one knows how or when these words might fit the circumstances of our day perfectly.

Two, the teachings are surprisingly common-sense, not heavily theological as we might expect. They stress the value of heartfelt counsel from a close friend (vv. 5–7), maintaining friendships, especially of neighbours (vv. 9–10), and taking good care of one's herds (vv. 23–27). When we read these verses, we might say, "That's just common sense." And it is—because the Bible is God's book, it is good to remember that common sense comes from God!

Three, this passage makes observations without offering solutions. What are we to do with a quarrelsome wife (vv. 15–16)? How can we satisfy our endless desires (v. 20)? How can we remove folly from the fool (v. 22)? When John Wesley, the founder of the Methodist church, asked his father Samuel which Bible commentary was the best to use, Samuel replied: "The Bible itself." **Likewise, when we are reading Proverbs and want to find a godly solution to these questions raised, we must turn to the full counsel of God's Word for guidance.**

What are we to do with a quarrelsome wife? Ephesians 5:25–28 notes that she is to be loved as Christ loves the church. How do we satisfy seemingly insatiable demands? Philippians 4:10–13 tells us that being in Christ is the key to the contented life. How can we rid a fool of his foolishness? 2 Corinthians 5:17 says that a person in Christ is a new creation, and John 3:1–15 tells us that we all need to be born again.

Proverbs 27:17 is a well-known proverb about the positive influence of a good friend. In the same way that iron rubbing against iron makes both sharper, mutual encouragement, teaching, and correction produce growth in wisdom and prepare us for life's challenges (see also Proverbs 13:20). We are image bearers of a God who relates, so we relate to one another. Hebrews 10:25 reminds us not to give up meeting together. Our churches are to be places of warm fellowship and positive influence, where we sharpen and spur one another on, so that it becomes, as theologian John Calvin put it: "the theatre in which the divine glory is displayed".

ThinkThrough

How does the prudence of Proverbs 27:12 show itself in verses 23–27?

How can you encourage the mutual sharpening mentioned in Proverbs 27:17 in your church, small group, and circle of fellow believers? How can you be a sharpening iron to others?

Day 41

Read Proverbs 28

While the last chapter largely contained practical insights and common-sense teachings, this chapter gives greater focus on the deeds of God's righteous people and how they will live in a covenant relationship with Him. Proverbs 28:1 tells us that the wicked flee—no doubt because of their sinful deeds—but the righteous are secure because of their relationship with God.

Verses 4 and 7 tell us how the righteous live—heeding God's instruction. Some Bible versions translate the word "instruction" as "law", reflecting some scholars' belief that the instruction here refers to the law that God gave His people after redeeming them at the Passover and delivering them from Egypt. The law showed them how they were to live as His redeemed people; obeying the law was not the way to earn redemption—"do this and live"—but the fruit of redemption—"live and do this".

Unlike those who mix with bad company (v. 7), the discerning son keeps the law. If we neglect the law, however, God will not hear us (v. 9). Our prayers become detestable because we are not hearing and obeying Him. Psalm 66:18, too, says: "If I had cherished sin in my heart, the Lord would not have listened." Obedience is never easy, nor is it always advantageous; it is thus an act of trust. **To trust in the Lord is to live in the fear of the Lord, walking in accordance with His ways and wisdom.** It also means listening to Him and being sensitive to sin, confessing and renouncing it instead of hiding it (Proverbs 28:13).

Trusting in the Lord and walking in His ways will lead to true prosperity and safety (vv. 18, 25–26). Those who do the opposite—hardening their hearts against God and pursuing a sinful life—will fall into trouble (vv. 14, 18). Verses 12 and 28 note that the character of leaders—whether good or evil—will have a great impact on the people under them. Today, the rejection of God and His ways shows itself in the lack of respect for life (murder), body (adultery), goods (stealing), reputation (false testimony), and self (covetous consumerism). Nations suffer when the wicked rise to positions of authority.

Our only hope is in the redemption that God alone gives. Only He can turn the wicked into the righteous, the disgraceful into the discerning, the troubled into the blessed, the perverse into the blameless, and the self-centred into the faithful. It is little wonder, therefore, that Paul calls Christ our wisdom from God— "our righteousness, holiness and redemption" (1 Corinthians 1:30).

What practical instructions does Proverbs 28 give on how we can live a righteous life (vv. 4–5, 7, 13–14, 25–26)? How can you put them into practice in your own life?

What would trusting in the Lord look like in your life?

Day 42

Read Proverbs 28

The poor, along with those who are weak and vulnerable, have always had a special place in God's heart. In the Bible, they are also often compared to the rich. Proverbs 28 makes six observations of the poor:

One, the poor are at the mercy of leaders, who can be a source of blessing or curse to them. Thoughtless policies can be devastating to the vulnerable, just as heavy rains can destroy crops (v. 3). Some Bible versions refer to a "poor man" oppressing the poor rather than a "ruler", reflecting a possible alternative translation of the original Hebrew word. In this case, the observation is of a poor man who oppresses the poor—even though we would expect him to have greater sympathy for his fellows.

Two, it is better to be poor and blameless and to keep one's integrity, than to be rich and crooked (v. 6). This verse stresses the value of integrity and virtue over wealth.

Three, the poor may suffer when the unrighteous seek to grow rich by charging them exorbitant interest. Ultimately, however, these rich people will not be able to hold onto their wealth, as it will end up in the hands of the virtuous who will distribute it back to the poor (v. 8). While this verse does not say how

this will happen, we can surmise that God, who cares for the poor and vulnerable, will ensure justice will prevail.

Four, the poor may possess a wealth of wisdom that the rich lack (v. 11). The rich may have a false sense of security and are blind to their true needs and condition, whereas the poor have the discernment to see wealth and arrogance for what they really are (see 23:5).

Five, poverty can also be a result of daydreaming—or hoping for shortcuts to wealth—instead of working hard (28:19). Or it can result from a selfish greed that will eventually lead to poverty (v. 22).

Six, generosity will be rewarded (v. 27; see also 11:24–25). **Our God is a generous God: He gives graciously, even though we do not deserve it and so, He expects us to show compassionate generosity too.** We give because God gave (2 Corinthians 8:7–9). This is why Israel was to recognise God's ownership and generosity by giving a tithe of 10 per cent. Without being legalistic, this is a good proportion for giving, though we ought to feel free to give much more.

Britain's great post-war builder John Laing, a man of firm Christian conviction, made millions from his construction company, but was known for his generosity. It was said of Laing that "the man who had handled millions had given them all away". Laing was also known for living frugally; he once said: "Everyone should have a home just big enough to serve its purpose."[8]

The sluggard never has anything to share; one of the blessings of work is that it gives us the opportunity to give. The three key points of a well-known sermon by the founder of the Methodist church, John Wesley, on the use of money were: earn all you can; give all you can; save all you can. Remember: "God loves a cheerful giver" (2 Corinthians 9:7).

[8] Garry J. Williams, *Silent Witnesses* (Edinburgh: Banner of Truth Publishers, 2013), 148–149.

ThinkThrough

Reflect on what Proverbs 28 says about the poor and the rich. How does it compare to your own views on wealth? And what would it say about your attitude towards your personal wealth and possessions?

How can you be more generous today? Think of some practical ways to give.

Day 43

Read Proverbs 29

Proverbs 29 is the last group of proverbs compiled by King Hezekiah's scribes (see day 37). Today, I want to highlight two pairs of proverbs and two individual proverbs.

Proverbs 29:2 and 16 contrast the effects of the righteous and wicked thriving. There is heartfelt joy in one and deep groaning in the other (v. 2). One upholds justice while the other does not care for it (v. 7). As a result, one will prevail and the other will be punished (v. 16).

Proverbs 29:15 and 17 stress the importance of disciplining children. All of us are sinful by nature and therefore, it takes correction and discipline to nurture a child who is not a disgrace to his parents (v. 15), and will instead bring joy and peace (v. 17; see also 22:15; 23:13–14). While physical cruelty and abuse is to be avoided, a total lack of the rod will lead to waywardness.

Proverbs 29:18 reminds us of the importance and value of God's Word in guiding us, without which we will go our sinful ways unrestrained. Heeding His instruction will bring blessing.

How grateful we can be that God has revealed to us His values and His ways in His Word! Imagine what a place the world would be without His guidance! English preacher Charles Spurgeon,

stressing the importance of prayerful study of God's revelation, noted that this was an act of devotion "wherein the transforming power of grace is often exercised, changing us into the image of Him of whom the Word is a mirror".[9]

Proverbs 29:25 notes that safety is found in trusting in the Lord (see also 18:10). If we trust in people instead of the Lord, we can fall into the trap of allowing them to gain power and influence over our lives—the fear of men will become a snare.

We need to remember that the Lord is ultimately in control of all things; He directs the heart of the king (Proverbs 21:1). This truth is perhaps the most comforting truth in the Bible—Romans 8:28 reminds us that God is not only in control of all things, but also that He exercises His control for our good. In the context of Romans 8, the "good", which is His goal, is that we should be conformed to the likeness of Jesus Christ (v. 29). **Everything that comes into our lives—whether good or bad—is designed or allowed by God to lead to our growth in godliness.**

Trust the One in control and do not fall into the trap of fearing people. As church father Augustine put it: "Nothing, therefore, happens unless the omnipotent wills it to happen: He either permits it to happen, or He brings it about Himself".[10]

[9] Steve Miller, *C.H. Spurgeon on Spiritual Leadership* (Chicago: Moody Publishers, 2008), 109.
[10] St. Augustine, *Faith, Hope and Charity*, trans. Louis A. Arand (New York: Paulist Press, 1947), 89.

ThinkThrough

Which of these four sets of proverbs do you find most encouraging and needful in your life right now? How can you apply it to your words, actions, and thoughts?

How has the knowledge of God's Word, instruction, and guidance (Proverbs 29:18) changed the way you live? What other changes do you think are needed?

Day 44

Read Proverbs 29

In Proverbs 29, we see the difference in lifestyle, actions, and attitude between those who choose wisdom and those who do not, and the results of their choice. They include:

- The man who seeks wisdom will be a blessing to his parents, but the man who rejects wisdom wastes his money on wild living (v. 3).

- The wise king who seeks to do right and rule justly will bring blessings to the nation, but the corrupt ruler will destroy it (v. 4).

- Those who choose evil will find themselves trapped by it, but those who choose wisdom will find joy (v. 6).

- Those who reject wisdom stir up trouble with their mocking and careless words, but the wise will bring peace (v. 8).

- Those who reject wisdom are filled with pride but will ultimately be brought low, while the wise remain humble and will ultimately be honoured (v. 23).

Besides contrasting the actions and fruit of those who choose or reject wisdom, Proverbs 29 also makes several observations about those who choose to live foolishly:

- Their stubbornness and repeated refusal to heed wise corrections will lead to their destruction (v. 1).

- Their use of flattery (perhaps to trap others) will eventually land them in a trap (v. 5).

- Those who choose evil will always be opposed to those who choose good (v. 10).

- The undiscerning ruler who does not seek to distinguish between truth and lies will breed corruption and evil (v. 12).

- The servant who is lazy, rebellious, or stubborn will not listen to verbal correction, and may need stronger discipline to make him turn away from his foolishness (v. 19).

- Impulsive, hasty speech make for fools of the worst kind (v. 20).

- Those who become accomplices in crime will find themselves in a bind when told to testify: either they tell the truth and incriminate themselves, or lie and break their oath (v. 24).

By contrasting the outcomes of those who live wisely and those who don't, and by showing us the consequences of those who live foolishly, Proverbs 29 makes clear what we should do—and should not do—to avoid living in a manner that contradicts God's ways. It ends with a strong note that the righteous and wicked will always be at odds with one another (v. 27). There is no middle ground.

This irreconcilable conflict between good and evil can be seen in the repeated use of the expression "the LORD detests" throughout Proverbs (3:32; 11:1, 20; 12:22; 15:8–9, 26; 17:15; 20:10, 23). **Just as the Lord detests evil, the wise will reflect His righteousness and detest all that is wicked too** (29:27).

In 2 Corinthians 6:14–18, Paul stresses the believer's solidarity with God, noting that righteousness and wickedness cannot have anything in common. He goes on to quote Leviticus 26:12 and Isaiah 52:11, which call us to walk in God's ways and to be holy, to separate ourselves from unrighteousness.

Jesus makes the same call. In John 8:44, He warns those living in solidarity with their father, the devil. In contrast, the family of God lives in solidarity with the Father and does the Father's will (Matthew 12:49–50).

ThinkThrough

Take another look at the contrasts between those who choose wisdom and those who do not in Proverbs 29. Which ones can you apply to your life?

What does it mean to be in union with Christ? What changes can you make to live in solidarity with Him and the Father's will?

Day 45

Read Proverbs 30:1–14

Who is Agur? Who is Ithiel? We know very little about these two people in Proverbs 30:1. Agur, son of Jakeh, is not mentioned anywhere else in the Bible, while Ithiel features only one other time, in Nehemiah 11:7. What we do know, however, is that Agur is a humble man, as evidenced by what he says to Ithiel in Proverbs 30:2–3.

In the Bible, wisdom teaching often begins with the writer encouraging his listener to heed his words of wisdom. Agur, however, begins by acknowledging his own ignorance and need for God's wisdom—which is the first step to receiving true insight from God.

In verse 4, Agur observes that no human can do what God alone has done. God's revelation of the truth, and His coming down to tell us that truth, is unique to the Christian faith. In John 3:12–13, the Lord Jesus says that He is the one who has come down to tell us of heavenly things. **Because the revelation of spiritual things comes from God himself—and not from man's discovery—we can be sure that this revelation is completely true and reliable.**

That's why Agur affirms that God's words are flawless (Proverbs 30:5–6). They are therefore the perfect source of wisdom, for they are adequate

and in no need of supplementing by so-called human wisdom, which is flawed. In fact, we are warned not to add to God's holy Word (v. 6; see also Revelation 22:18–19).

Agur thus asks God to keep him from falsehood, and to grant him contentment and a life of moderation (Proverbs 30:7–8). The wise man knows that extreme wealth might lead him to forget his dependence on God, while extreme poverty might tempt him to steal (v. 9). Both requests—to glorify God's name and to be contented with one's daily bread—will feature again in the prayer that Jesus teaches us in Matthew 6:9 and 11.

In Proverbs 30:10, Agur warns against meddling in others' affairs by making false accusations against a servant to his master. This, he notes, will earn a deserved curse from the master.

In verses 11–14, Agur goes on to list four character traits or actions of the proud that should be avoided:

- **Dishonouring one's parents (v. 11).** The fifth commandment makes clear that we are to honour our parents (Exodus 20:12), while Exodus 21:17 and Proverbs 30:17 give clear warnings against mocking and scorning our parents.

- **Hypocrisy (v. 12).** The proud believe themselves to be righteous, and are blind to their own sin.

- **Arrogance (v. 13).** The proud look down on others, believing themselves to be superior above all.

- **Cruelty and greed (v. 14).** The proud seek to destroy with their words and actions, and to exploit the poor and needy.

Christian writer C. S. Lewis called pride "the complete anti-God state of mind",[11] while church reformist John Calvin described it as the twin of unbelief in God.[12] The ugliness of pride is seen in its lack of respect for those closest to us, in its ignorance of one's own faults, in its arrogance, and in its hardness towards those in need. In contrast, a genuine belief and trust in God leads to humility and compassion, for we will realise our complete dependence on Him and know that we are to care for others.

[11] C. S. Lewis, *Mere Christianity*.
[12] John Calvin, *John Calvin's Complete Commentary on the Bible* (Harrington, DE: Delmarva Publications, 2013).

ThinkThrough

Agur shows great humility and awareness of his sin and needs (Proverbs 30:2–3). How does his attitude compare with yours? Ask God to help you to be honest in your assessment of your attitude in the light of God's Word.

Reflect on Agur's descriptions of pride. Could any of them be said of your thoughts, words, or actions?

Day 46

Read Proverbs 30:15–33

Agur has a wonderful capacity for observation. He sees with the wide-eyed wonder of a child, yet his observations are mature and insightful. He is a keen observer of life, and invites us to reflect with him. Today, we look at some of Agur's "lists" in Proverbs 30.

In verse 15, he warns us about the insatiable appetite of greed, aptly illustrated by the leech whose two daughters live off others' blood and yet are never satisfied. This theme leads us to the observation of four other things that are never satisfied (v. 16): the grave's hunger for the dead; the womb that is created to carry children but remains empty; the arid land that needs more water; and fire, which never stops its search for combustibles. While two of these examples have to do with destruction (death and fire) and two with the giving of life (birth and water), they illustrate the principle that there is always a desire that can never be satisfied.

In verses 18–19, Agur gives another list, this time of four things that mystify him: How does the eagle stay up in the sky? How does the snake move so quickly even though it has no legs? How is a large ship able to float when a small pebble sinks? How does one account for love between a man and a woman? The mystery and wonder of these four things—especially the last,

of love between a man and woman—form a stark contrast with the blatant, unrepentant ways of the adulteress (v. 20). Her casual approach to sex outside marriage, and her loss of all moral awareness, invoke horror rather than amazement.

Continuing on this theme, Agur goes on to list four injustices that upset the order of things and lead to dire consequences (vv. 21–23): a servant who rules even though he is unfit; a fool who is rewarded despite his godlessness; an unlovable woman who marries—and who will probably wreak terror on her husband; and the maid who by some means takes over her mistress' position. These examples involve the rewarding of foolishness and vice, and upsetting of the natural order of society.

Next, Agur lists four small creatures that exemplify wisdom (vv. 24–28). Wisdom is not necessarily tied to physical strength or size. Here are four small animals—ants, hyraxes, locusts, and lizards—that live wisely and successfully. Ants plan for their future, hyraxes ensure their security, locusts organise themselves, and lizards know the best place to live.

This list is followed by another list of four stately animals or men (vv. 29–31): the lion, the rooster, the goat, and the strong king.

Agur concludes his observations with this warning in verses 32–33: evil schemes and stirring up anger will lead to strife as surely as butter emerges from milk and blood from a twisted nose. Bible commentator Derek Kidner sums up Proverbs 30 as a call by Agur for humility through reverence (vv. 1–9), restraint (vv. 10–17), wonder (vv. 18–31), and peaceable behaviour (vv. 32–33).[13]

Reflect on Agur's observations on greed, and think about your own desires, needs, and wants, and how they can be satisfied. How can you apply Agur's lessons to your life?

Close your mouth, give up your petty scheming, and seek the wisdom of the One who is all-wise. Wonder at His creation and His wisdom in sending His Son to open the way to the new creation!

What kind of petty scheming might we be involved in? How can we examine our thoughts, plans, and intentions in the light of God's Word?

[13] Derek Kidner, *Proverbs*, Tyndale Old Testament Commentaries (Nottingham, UK: Inter-Varsity Press, 1964).

Day 47

Read Proverbs 31:1–9

This final section of Proverbs is attributed to King Lemuel. We don't know much about who Lemuel was and where he reigned. Lemuel, which means "belonging to God", is mentioned only once in the Bible, though some scholars believe it was a pen name for another king, possibly Solomon or Hezekiah.

Lemuel's sayings are presented as a teaching from his mother and can be divided into two sections: advice for the king on ruling and administering justice (Proverbs 31:2–9), and a description of an excellent wife (vv. 10–31). Today, we look at Lemuel's mother's advice on what he should not do (vv. 3–7) and what he should do (vv. 8–9).

First, Lemuel is to avoid giving in to the temptations of unrestrained sexual gratification (v. 3) and drink (v. 4–7)—two temptations very real to a man with power and money.

The instruction not to "spend your strength on women" (v. 3) echoes the warning given to kings in Deuteronomy 17:17: a king must not take many wives, for they will lead him astray. This was Solomon's downfall. Immorality is not conducive to wise rule, for the king is God's representative and is to be a man of integrity; there is to be no distinction between the king's public and private life (Proverbs 5–7).

Addiction to alcohol is also not conducive to wise rule (Proverbs 31:4–5), as it will deprive the king of a clear mind needed to make wise decisions. Wine and beer can cause kings to forget or neglect their lawful duty to protect society's most vulnerable (v. 5), who have no one else to depend on. Unlike those who are suffering or in anguish, the king is not to resort to drinking to forget his woes (vv. 6–7), for he needs to be ever alert.

Second, Lemuel is to protect the poor, the needy, and the oppressed (vv. 8–9) by speaking up for them and judging fairly. The poor and the destitute cannot afford a bribe or an advocate, so the king must defend their rights (see 16:12). As his words are highly influential (16:10) and taken as law, the king has a special responsibility to look out for those with the least influence.

King Lemuel's mother's advice is just as applicable to us today, whether or not we are in a position of leadership or influence. We can also pray for our leaders to heed these wise words. As preacher Peter Marshall, a former Chaplain to the American Senate, once prayed for leaders: "Let no personal ambition blind them to their opportunities.

Help them to give battle to hypocrisy wherever they find it. Give them divine common sense and a selflessness that shall make them think of service and not of gain."[14]

[14] Catherine Marshall, ed., *The Prayers of Peter Marshall* (New York: McGraw-Hill Book Company, 1985).

What influence do you have in your community, workplace, and family? Within your sphere of influence, how can you look out for the interests of the poor and needy around you?

How can you pray for your leaders in your nation, workplace, and church today?

Day 48

Read Proverbs 31:10–31

The book of Proverbs concludes with this beautifully constructed acrostic poem, in which each verse begins with the succeeding letter of the Hebrew alphabet.

This poem (Proverbs 31:10–31) praises the wife of noble character. It stresses her inestimable value, noting that she must be searched for ("who can find?", v. 10). To discover a woman such as this is a cause for thanksgiving.

The wife of noble character is a diligent homemaker, getting up before dawn to provide for her whole household (v. 15), making high-quality clothing for them (vv. 13, 21), and efficiently managing their affairs (v. 27). But she is not just a stay-at-home mum. She also has considerable business acumen, developing land (v. 16), trading profitably (v. 18), and making and selling clothing (v. 24). There is no idleness about her (v. 27); she thinks of every provision for the future, so that she never has to worry about what might happen (v. 25).

As a result, her husband has great confidence in her, for she is completely reliable and frees him up for his own duties (v. 11). He lacks nothing he needs and is respected among the elders (v. 23). He praises her, realising how fortunate he is (v. 28).

Typical of the wise, the wife of noble character does not hoard her wealth, but shares it generously (v. 20), using her prosperity to help the poor and needy.

All this activity is an outflow of what the wife of noble character is within. She is strong and dignified (v. 25), and wise and faithful in her teaching (v. 26). **The wife of noble character displays all the characteristics of wisdom which are taught throughout Proverbs—and which are therefore also applicable to men.**

Mothers, especially, will find great encouragement in this chapter. In investing so much of their time and effort—and themselves—in their children, they make great sacrifices; their long days never seem to end, and much of their effort often goes unacknowledged. Proverbs 31:10–31, however, gives the assurance that all their efforts will ultimately be rewarded. They will be recognised and praised, just as the wife of noble character is praised by her children and husband, who recognise how blessed they have been to have been nurtured by such a mother and wife (v. 28–29): "Many women do noble things, but you surpass them all."

Finally, the wife of noble character is praised for her fear of the Lord (v. 30), for putting her trust in the God who placed her in her family.

A prayer for families in *The Minister's Service Handbook* says: "Grant unto us a revival of the simplicity and purity of home life; parents raising children in the love and nurture of the Lord and children loving and respecting parents; stir up in the young a zeal for that which is honourable and good; strengthen the middle aged to be persistently diligent in the living and teaching values of integrity; and keep the hearts of the aged in quiet trust that their eventide may be light."[15]

[15] James L. Christensen, *The Minister's Service Handbook* (Grand Rapids, MI: Fleming H. Revell, 1960), 128.

How can you apply the traits of the wife of noble character to your own life and family?

Commit yourself to praying for your family today, and ask God to help you and your family honour Him in your family life.

Day 49

Read Proverbs 31:10–31

In this portrait of a remarkable woman, Proverbs 31:30 provides the key to her noble character and activities: all she does flows out from who she is—"a woman who fears the LORD". Charm can be a covering and outer beauty can come and go; for this woman, however, no matter her age or mood, reverence for God will be the persistent, lifelong motivating factor in life.

So the book of Proverbs ends as it began, stressing reverence for God (1:7 and 31:30) as the beginning of knowledge and the motivation for the lifestyle of righteousness.

Scientific study, which is based on experiment and observation, does not yield answers to life's biggest questions like: "Who am I?", "Why am I here?", "What is life about?", and "Where am I going?" Science cannot answer these questions conclusively as they fall outside the field of experiment and observation; only God can, so we rely on revelation—His Word—to give us understanding. We learn to interpret all of life through the lens of His Word, the Bible.

Throughout this book, our definition of wisdom has been living according to God's ways. This means not ignoring, mocking, or trying to manipulate Him, but revering and trusting Him.

True wisdom means fearing the Lord and living according to His purpose. God's purpose is to glorify himself as both Creator and Redeemer: He is the Owner, first by right of creation, and then again by right of purchase, which He paid for with the life and death of His Son, the Lord Jesus Christ. It is in understanding the purpose of God that we have the answers to these bigger questions.

In New Testament terms, the life of wisdom is the life that is lived in Christ, who is God's wisdom in the flesh (John 1:14). This life is one that is lived in repentance and faith towards God, and in harmony with His plan for dealing with sin and bringing in the new creation. As twice-owned people belonging to God by right of creation and by right of redemption, we are to live a redeemed lifestyle patterned after Jesus' life and in accordance with the exhortations of the New Testament.

By thy blood, O spotless lamb,
Shed so willingly for me,
Let my heart be all thine own,
Let me live to thee alone.
—F. R. Havergal

ThinkThrough

Read through Proverbs 31:10–31 again. How does the woman of noble character show wisdom in the way she lives?

Reflect on your own life and your activities. How do they compare to those of the woman of noble character? How can you show wisdom in your life?

Day 50

Read 1 Kings 3:1–28

I want to conclude this book on Proverbs, a remarkable book of wisdom, with a warning. Let's take a deeper look at Solomon, the son of David, the king of Israel who wrote most of Proverbs.

In the early chapters of 1 Kings, we get an insight into Solomon's administration, achievements, and especially his wisdom. God tells him: "I will give you a wise and discerning heart, so that there will never have been anyone like you, nor will there ever be" (1 Kings 3:12). But in 11:1 we are told that "King Solomon, however, loved many foreign women". This was clearly contrary to God's instruction: "You must not intermarry with them, because they will surely turn your hearts after their gods" (v. 2).

Much of Solomon's God-given wisdom is recorded in the book of Proverbs. So how could he have gone so wrong?

Solomon's life is a warning to us. It is one thing to know and write about God's wisdom, and quite another to live by it, to maintain one's fear of the Lord in the midst of the pleasures and pressures of life. For Solomon, pride proved to be the biggest enemy.

How hard it must have been for Solomon to remain humble when he was surrounded by the adoration of so many seeking his counsel! The Queen of Sheba, for example, was one of many rulers impressed by Solomon's wisdom (10:6–9). It must have tempted him to take his wisdom for granted and believe that it was a natural talent rather than a gift of God.

There was also his wealth, as described in 1 Kings 4:20–28. Along with his wisdom, Solomon's wealth was given by God: "I will give you what you have not asked for—both wealth and honour" (3:13). But Solomon in his wealth forgot the Lord (see Proverbs 30:9).

To be wise includes knowing where one's strength— and limits—lies. It means acknowledging that our true sufficiency lies in God, that we need to depend totally on Him.

Power, wealth, and popularity are a powerful cocktail and fuel for human pride. Solomon had all three, and they turned out to be his downfall. He thought he knew better than God and allowed himself to be led by his pride. "So Solomon did evil in the eyes of the LORD; he did not follow the LORD completely, as David his father had done" (1 Kings 11:6).

There is another king, however, who remained humble and obedient despite having all power and wisdom (see Matthew 13:54; Colossians 2:3). There was no pride in the Lord Jesus, and His life was pure integrity.

To come to Christ is to embrace God's wisdom. To follow Christ is to live the truly wise life!

What gifts and talents have God given you? How can you use them for His glory while reminding yourself to rely completely on Him?

Read Proverbs 1:7 and 31:30 again. Reflect on these verses, memorise them, and make a fresh commitment to fear the Lord, for this is the beginning of wisdom.

Journey Through

Acts

The book of Acts is one of the most exciting parts of the Bible. Jesus has just ascended to heaven, the Spirit has come to the church, and we see God at work building the church and causing the gospel message to spread through Judea, into Samaria, throughout Asia, into Europe, and finally to Rome. Embark on a daily journey through the book of Acts, and see how the Holy Spirit empowers the church to witness in ever widening circles until the gospel reaches the ends of the earth.

David Cook was Principal of the Sydney Missionary and Bible College for 26 years. He is an accomplished writer and has authored Bible commentaries, books on the Minor Prophets, and several Bible study guides.

Journey Through

Judges

The book of Judges describes a low point in the history of God's people. It tells of a time of moral and spiritual anarchy, when everyone ignored God's life-giving laws and did what they thought was right in their own eyes. It is a story of disobedience and defeat. Yet the book also contains glimpses of the Israelites' capacity for greatness—when they chose to trust and depend on God. Discover God's great principles of life, and find out how we can lead powerful, productive lives in a society that is increasingly hostile to our faith.

Gary Inrig is a graduate of the University of British Columbia and Dallas Theological Seminary. An established Bible teacher and former pastor, he has authored several books, including *True North*, *The Parables*, *Forgiveness*, and *Whole Marriages in a Broken World*.

Journey Through

Hosea

As God's spokesman, Hosea is told by Him to marry Gomer, a prostitute, and to go again and again to woo her back despite her many infidelities. Hosea's commitment to love Gomer gives us a glimpse of God's love for us. God loves His people as passionately and as jealously as a devoted husband loves his wife. Even when we wander from Him and our hearts cool towards Him, He continues to come after us and to draw us back to Him. God's love will never let us go. Rekindle your love and commitment to the One who loves you!

David Gibb is the former Vicar of St. Andrew's Church in Leyland and Honorary Canon of Blackburn Cathedral. He is committed to training church planters and gospel workers, and is one of the contributors to a new NIV Study Bible. He is also author of a book on Revelation.

For information on our resources, visit **ourdailybread.org**. Alternatively, please contact the office nearest you from the list below, or go to **ourdailybread.org/locations** for the complete list of offices.

BELARUS
Our Daily Bread Ministries
PO Box 82, Minsk, Belarus 220107
belarus@odb.org • (375-17) 2854657; (375-29) 9168799

GERMANY
Our Daily Bread Ministries e.V.
Schulstraße 42, 79540 Lörrach
deutsch@odb.org

IRELAND
Our Daily Bread Ministries
64 Baggot Street Lower, Dublin 2, D02 XC62
ireland@odb.org • +3531 (01) 676 7315

RUSSIA
MISSION Our Daily Bread
PO Box "Our Daily Bread",
str.Vokzalnaya 2, Smolensk, Russia 214961
russia@odb.org • 8(4812)660849; +7(951)7028049

UKRAINE
Christian Mission Our Daily Bread
PO Box 533, Kiev, Ukraine 01004
ukraine@odb.org • +380964407374; +380632112446

UNITED KINGDOM (Europe Regional Office)
Our Daily Bread Ministries
PO Box 1, Millhead, Carnforth, LA5 9ES
europe@odb.org • +44 (0)15395 64149

ourdailybread.org

Sign up to *Journey Through*

We would love to support you with the *Journey Through* series! Please be aware we can only provide one copy of each future *Journey Through* book per reader (previous books from the series are available to purchase).

If you know of other people who would be interested in this series, we can send you introductory *Journey Through* booklets to pass onto them (which include details on how they can easily sign up for the books themselves).

☐ **I would like to regularly receive the *Journey Through* series**

☐ **Please send me ____ copies of the *Journey Through* introductory booklet**

Just complete and return this sign up form to us at:

Our Daily Bread Ministries, PO Box 1, Millhead, Carnforth, LA5 9ES, United Kingdom

Here at Our Daily Bread Ministries we take your privacy seriously. We will only use this personal information to manage your account, and regularly provide you with *Journey Through* series books and offers of other resources, three ministry update letters each year, and occasional additional mailings with news that's relevant to you. We will also send you ministry updates and details of Discovery House products by email if you agree to this. In order to do this we share your details with our UK-based mailing house and Our Daily Bread Ministries in the US. We do not sell or share personal information with anyone for marketing purposes.

Please do not complete and sign this form for anyone but yourself. You do not need to complete this form if you already receive regular copies of *Journey Through* from us.

Full Name (Mr/Mrs/Miss/Ms): _____

Address: _____

_____

Postcode: _____ Tel: _____

Email: _____
☐ I would like to receive email updates and details of Discovery House products.

Signature: _____

All our resources, including *Journey Through*, are available without cost. Many people, making even the smallest of donations, enable Our Daily Bread Ministries to reach others with the life-changing wisdom of the Bible. We are not funded or endowed by any group or denomination.